MANAGERIAL CHALLENGES

IN THE LIGHT OF

SOCIO-MATHEMATICAL FUZZY SYSTEMS & MATHEMATICAL FUZZINESS

Dr. Dhinesha Ruwanthi Perera

Senior Lecturer

Department of Management and Finance

General Sir John Kotelawala Defence University

Sri Lanka

dhinesha_drp@kdu.ac.lk

Rakesh M. Patel

Department of Mathematics

Government Science College

Gandhinagar, Gujarat, India

rmpatel2711@gmail.com

DIAMOND BOOKS

www.diamondbooks.in

Publisher : **Diamond Pocket Books (P) Ltd.**
X-30, Okhla Industrial Area,
Phase-II, New Delhi-110020
Phone : 011-40712200
E-mail : wecare@diamondbooks.in
Website : www.diamondbooks.in
Edition : 2026
Printed By : Repro (India)

Managerial Challenges in the Light of Socio-Mathematical Fuzzy Systems & Mathematical Fuzziness
Author - *Dr. Dhinesha Ruwanthi Perera and Rakesh M. Patel*

TO PARENTS

Air Chief Marshal
Donald Perera

Air Commodore (Dr)
Ranjani Perera

For their enthusiasm, guidance, continual encouragement and support

&

Dedicated to My Beloved Parents,
Jashodaben Manilal Patel
Manilal Harjivandas Patel

Who reside in their heavenly abode.

Keywords

Fuzzy Mathematics; Socio-Mathematics; Managerial Decision-Making; Fuzzy Logic; Uncertainty Modeling; Organizational Behavior; Fuzzy Sets; Soft Computing; Managerial Fuzziness; Linguistic Variables; Decision Support Systems.

Subject Classification

- Fuzzy Mathematics (Real-Life Ambiguity Modeling)
- Socio-Mathematics (Human–Social Behavior Quantification)
- Managerial Science (Practical Organizational Decisions)
- Decision Theory (Daily & Corporate Choice-Making)
- Uncertainty Modeling (Vague & Incomplete Data Handling)
- Fuzzy Logic & Soft Computing (AI-Driven Approximate Reasoning)
- Organizational Behavior (Human Interactions & Dynamics)
- Computational Decision Support (Digital Tools for Managers)
- Strategic Planning & Resource Allocation (Practical Use of Resources)
- Risk Analysis & Assessment (Real-World Risk Evaluation)
- Human-Centric Management Models (Behavior-Aligned Decision Systems)

FRONTISPIECE

"In the twilight zones of human decision-making—where precision fades and ambiguity begins— Fuzzy Mathematics becomes not merely a tool, but a philosophy for navigating managerial reality." Modern managerial environments are rarely crisp. They are shaped by **uncertainty, human behaviour, socio-cultural dynamics, incomplete information, and shifting organizational priorities**. Within this complex landscape, traditional binary logic offers only limited guidance. **Socio-Mathematical Fuzzy Theory** emerges as a bridge between **mathematical rigor and human-centric management**, enabling leaders to interpret shades of meaning, degrees of truth, and layers of complexity that define real-world decisions. This work highlights how **mathematical fuzziness** enriches managerial thought by offering:

- **Flexible reasoning models** for uncertain environments
- **Human-aligned decision systems** reflecting emotions, perceptions, and social influence
- **Soft computing approaches** for complex managerial problems
- **Frameworks for adaptive strategy, planning, and risk assessment**
- **Tools for exploring imprecision in human behaviour, negotiation, leadership, and organizational dynamics**

In this synthesis of **management science, fuzzy logic, and socio-mathematical analysis**, readers are invited to view managerial challenges not as rigid problems demanding definitive answers, but as **dynamic systems requiring graded understanding, multi-valued logic, and contextual intelligence**. Ultimately, this Frontispiece celebrates the idea that: **"Managers who understand fuzziness understand reality itself."**

Foreword

In today's world of uncertainty, rapid change, and complex decision-making, effective management is more essential than ever. Traditional quantitative approaches alone are no longer sufficient. Managers now require tools that embrace ambiguity, human behavioural nuances, and the socio-cultural forces shaping organisational life. *"Managerial Challenges in the Light of Socio-Mathematical Fuzzy Logic and Mathematical Fuzziness"* offers a timely response to these evolving needs.

Fuzzy mathematics—well known for modelling imprecision—provides a powerful lens for examining managerial issues with greater depth. By integrating socio-mathematical perspectives, the authors skillfully connect human-centred organisational behaviour with the structure of computational decision-support systems. This fusion equips readers with robust frameworks for handling uncertainty, evaluating complex decisions, and designing adaptive strategies.

The strength of this book lies in both its theoretical insight and practical application. From resource allocation to risk assessment, the tools presented here support clearer judgement, humane leadership, and strategic resilience.

I commend the authors for their rigorous scholarship and meaningful contribution to contemporary management research. This work will undoubtedly inspire further exploration and innovation in the field.

Extending my warm regards to you both, with heartfelt wishes for a bright and successful future in research.

-Dr. Dilip Rana Sir

Commissioner, The Office of the
Commissioner of Higher education,
2nd Floor, Block No. 12, Dr. Jivraj Mehta,
Gandhinagar, Gujarat, India.

Foreword

In an era defined by uncertainty, rapid transformation, and increasingly complex decision landscapes, the role of effective management has become more vital than ever before. Traditional quantitative methods, though valuable, can no longer fully capture the ambiguity, human variability, and socio-cultural dynamics that permeate modern organizations.

Managerial Challenges in the Light of Socio-Mathematical Fuzzy Logic and Mathematical Fuzziness offers a forward-looking and insightful response to these contemporary challenges. By harnessing the power of fuzzy mathematics—long recognised for its ability to model vagueness and imprecision—the authors illuminate managerial issues with remarkable clarity and depth. Their integration of socio-mathematical thinking further bridges the gap between human-centred organisational behaviour and systematic, computational decision-support frameworks.

This thoughtful fusion enables readers to navigate uncertainty with confidence, evaluate multifaceted decisions more effectively, and design strategies that remain adaptive and resilient. The true strength of this work lies not only in its theoretical sophistication but also in its practical relevance. Whether addressing resource allocation, leadership dynamics, or risk management, the methods and perspectives offered here provide managers and scholars alike with tools for more grounded judgement and humane, context-aware decision-making.

We applaud the authors for their intellectual rigor and their meaningful contribution to the evolution of contemporary management thought. Their work stands as both an inspiration and an invitation to further inquiry and innovation in this emerging interdisciplinary space.

With warm regards and deep appreciation, I extend my best wishes to the authors for continued success and a bright future in their research pursuits.

With warm regards and heartfelt wishes from both authors to the readers and the research community, may you thrive in knowledge, discovery, and scholarly impact.

-Dr. Dhinesha Ruwanthi Perera
Sri Lanka

-Rakesh Manilal Harjivandas Patel,
Gujarat, India

Acknowledgment

Sincere gratitude is extended to **Dr. Dilip Rana, Commissioner,** The Office of the Commissioner of Higher Education, Gandhinagar, for valuable guidance and encouragement that have significantly contributed to the development of this work.

Special appreciation is expressed to **Dr. Dhinesha Ruwanthi Perera** for expert insights, guidance, and support throughout the study. Her extensive knowledge in socio-mathematical modeling and fuzzy logic has enriched the depth and scope of the research.

Acknowledgment is also due to colleagues, peers, and participants who provided practical insights, suggestions, and feedback, enhancing the applicability of the research findings in real-life managerial contexts.

Finally, gratitude is extended to family and friends for their patience, encouragement, and moral support, which were vital throughout the research process.

This work is dedicated to scholars and practitioners striving to understand and manage the complexities of organizational decision-making under conditions of uncertainty.

With Regards… … …

-Dr. Dhinesha Ruwanthi Perera,
Sri Lanka
-Rakesh Manilal Harjivandas Patel,
Gujarat, India.

Eminent Reviewers

- **Dr. Sanjeev Kumar:** Vice Chancellor M S D Azamgarh
- **Dr. Harshad Patel:** Head, Department of Mathematics, Ganpat University, Kherba
- **Dr. Sanjay Choudhry:** Head, Department of Mathematics,
- **Dr. Narendra Kumar:** Department of Management, University of Noida
- **Dr. Rajesh K. Pandey:** Department of Mathematics, Indian Institute of Technology, Varanasi
- **Dr. Raya Karla Raya:** Department of Management, Tashkend University, Uzbekistan

Prologue

In an era defined by rapid technological advancement, globalization, and unprecedented levels of uncertainty, managerial decision-making has become increasingly complex. Traditional approaches, while valuable, often fall short in capturing the nuances of human behavior, organizational dynamics, and socio-cultural influences that shape real-world outcomes.

This work explores the intersection of socio-mathematical modeling and fuzzy mathematical logic to provide a deeper understanding of managerial challenges. By embracing the inherent ambiguity and imprecision of organizational environments, it seeks to offer frameworks and tools that enhance decision-making, strategic planning, and risk assessment.

The insights presented here are not limited to theoretical constructs; they aim to bridge the gap between abstract modeling and practical application. By integrating fuzzy logic with socio-mathematical approaches, this study provides a novel perspective on managing uncertainty, improving organizational efficiency, and fostering human-centric management practices.

This prologue sets the stage for a journey into the complex, often paradoxical world of management where mathematics, human behavior, and uncertainty converge. It invites readers—scholars, practitioners, and decision-makers alike—to explore new paradigms and rethink traditional frameworks in the light of mathematical fuzziness and socio-mathematical insight.

Short Summary

The increasing complexity of managerial environments—characterized by uncertainty, imprecision, human subjectivity, socio-behavioral variability, and evolving data ecosystems—demands mathematical tools capable of capturing real-world ambiguity. Socio-mathematical and fuzzy mathematical frameworks provide powerful mechanisms for modeling such fuzziness, enabling managers to analyze decisions under incomplete, vague, or conflicting information. This paper explores the intersection of managerial science, socio-mathematical structures, and fuzzy logic–based formalisms, identifying contemporary challenges in decision-making, strategic planning, resource allocation, risk assessment, and performance evaluation. Emphasis is placed on how linguistic variables, membership functions, fuzzy sets, fuzzy inference systems, and socio-mathematical constructs contribute to more adaptive and human-aligned managerial models. The study highlights managerial fuzziness as not merely a limitation but an inherent feature of socio-organizational behavior, offering pathways toward more resilient, transparent, and computation-assisted decision systems.

Preface

In today's rapidly evolving organizational landscape, managers face unprecedented challenges driven by uncertainty, technological advancement, globalization, and human behavioral complexity. Traditional quantitative approaches, while valuable, often fail to fully account for the ambiguity and imprecision inherent in real-world decision-making. This book addresses this gap by exploring the integration of socio-mathematical modeling and fuzzy mathematical frameworks in managerial practice.

The central premise of this work is that organizational decision-making can be better understood—and more effectively guided—by embracing the inherent fuzziness of human behavior and complex social interactions. By combining insights from socio-mathematics with the principles of fuzzy logic, this study provides a comprehensive approach to modeling, analyzing, and managing uncertainty in organizational contexts.

This book is designed for scholars, researchers, and practitioners who seek to understand the nuanced dynamics of management under uncertainty. It bridges theory and practice, offering not only conceptual frameworks but also actionable strategies to enhance decision-making, strategic planning, risk assessment, and human-centric management.

The chapters that follow present a structured exploration of managerial challenges, from foundational concepts to advanced modeling techniques, enriched with practical examples and real-world applications. It is hoped that this work will inspire further research, foster innovative management practices, and contribute meaningfully to the evolving field of decision science.

Gratitude is extended to all who have contributed their knowledge, insights, and encouragement throughout the development of this book. Their support has been instrumental in shaping a work that seeks to advance both the theory and practice of management in the age of complexity and uncertainty.

Contents

Chapter 1

Foundations of Modelling in Management & Commerce

Keywords: Modelling frameworks, decision science, quantitative analysis, business analytics, managerial decision-making, systems thinking, modelling lifecycle.

Subject Classification:

- **JEL:** C10 (General Econometric and Statistical Methods), M10 (General Management)
- **MSC:** 91B38 (Production models), 90Bxx (Operations research)
- **ACM CCS:** Applied computing → Business analytics

1.1 Introduction

Management and commerce modelling refers to the systematic use of conceptual, quantitative, and computational tools that describe, analyze, and improve business operations and strategic decisions. In a world characterized by digital transformation, global competition, and heightened customer expectations, modeling provides both clarity and precision. It allows managers to reduce uncertainty, simulate alternative scenarios, and select strategies that maximize value. Effective models translate complex realities—the behaviour of markets, customers, employees, financial flows, and supply chains—into structured representations that support decision-making. This chapter presents the theoretical foundations of modelling in management and commerce, setting the stage for deeper exploration of quantitative and qualitative models in later chapters.

1.2 Meaning of Modelling in Management

Modelling is the act of creating simplified representations of real-world business environments to understand, predict, or shape outcomes. A model abstracts essential elements of a business system while ignoring extraneous complexities.

Types of business phenomena captured by models:

- **Processes:** e.g., flow of materials in manufacturing, service workflows in retail.
- **Structures:** e.g., organizational hierarchies, market segmentation frameworks.
- **Behaviours:** e.g., customer purchasing patterns, employee productivity.
- **Financial dynamics:** e.g., cash flow patterns, profit projection models.

Forms of models:

1. **Qualitative models:**
    - Conceptual diagrams, frameworks (e.g., Porter's Five Forces).
    - Useful when data is limited or when exploring strategic issues.
2. **Quantitative models:**
    - Mathematical, statistical, or econometric formulations.
    - Employed in forecasting, optimization, financial analysis.

3. **Computational models:**
   - Simulations (e.g., Monte Carlo), agent-based models, machine learning.
   - Benefit from large datasets and computational power.

Each type plays a unique role in managerial decision-making, depending on data availability, decision context, and organizational needs.

1.3 Importance of Modelling in Management and Commerce

Modelling is indispensable for effective business leadership. Its importance can be understood through various managerial benefits.

1.3.1 Enhances Decision Quality

Managers face complex decisions involving uncertainty, multiple criteria, and resource constraints. Models help by:

- Structuring problems,
- Comparing alternative decisions,
- Reducing human bias,
- Making assumptions explicit.

Examples:

Pricing models, capital budgeting analysis, resource allocation models.

1.3.2 Predicts Future Outcomes

Forecasting models estimate:

- Customer demand,
- Costs and revenues,
- Market trends,
- Economic conditions.

Accurate predictions enable better production planning, staffing, budgeting, and investment decisions.

1.3.3 Increases Efficiency and Productivity

Models reveal inefficiencies and bottlenecks in operations, allowing organizations to:

- Reduce cycle time,
- Improve resource utilization,
- Optimize supply chains,
- Implement automation.

For example, queuing models enhance service efficiency; layout models improve factory operations.

1.3.4 Supports Strategic Planning

Strategic models enable long-term thinking by helping managers:

- Test "what-if" scenarios,
- Evaluate competitive threats,
- Assess potential market entry strategies.

Scenario modelling and game theory frameworks strengthen strategic foresight.

1.3.5 Enhances Communication

Visual representations—graphs, flowcharts, dashboards—make complex business issues understandable across departments. This improves collaboration and reduces misinterpretation.

1.4 Characteristics of Effective Management Models

An effective model must balance simplicity with relevance. Key characteristics include:

- **Simplicity:** Eliminates unnecessary details to reduce cognitive load.
- **Logical structure:** Clear cause–effect relationships among variables.
- **Quantifiability:** Supports objective measurement and analysis where possible.
- **Flexibility:** Adaptable to new data, changed assumptions, or dynamic environments.
- **Realism:** Mirrors actual business constraints and behaviours.
- **Predictive ability:** Provides reliable insights about future states.

These features determine whether a model is truly useful for managerial decision-making.

1.5 Types of Models Used in Commerce and Management

Different business problems require different modelling approaches.

1.5.1 Descriptive Models

Explain how systems **currently operate** without recommending actions.

- Process maps for operational workflows.
- Organizational charts depicting reporting relationships.
- Value stream maps in lean management.

Use cases: diagnosing inefficiencies, training employees, documenting processes.

1.5.2 Predictive Models

- Forecast future outcomes under certain assumptions.

- Demand forecasting using time-series analysis.
- Regression-based sales or cost models.
- Customer churn prediction.

These models help anticipate trends and prepare for upcoming changes.

1.5.3 Prescriptive Models

Recommend **optimal decisions** using optimization or decision rules.

Examples:

- Linear programming for production mix decisions.
- Decision trees for evaluating choices under uncertainty.
- Inventory models such as EOQ.

Widely used in supply chains, finance, and operations management.

1.5.4 Conceptual Models

High-level analytical tools used to interpret strategic and qualitative issues.

- SWOT Analysis for internal and external assessments.
- Balanced Scorecard for performance management.
- Porter's Five Forces for competitive analysis.

They help managers understand underlying drivers of business performance.

1.6 Systems Thinking in Management Modelling

Systems thinking approaches organizations as complex, interconnected entities rather than isolated units. It emphasizes relationships, feedback loops, and emergent behaviour.

Core principles:

1. **Holism:** Solutions require understanding the whole system, not isolated components.
2. **Interdependence:** Changes in one part affect others (e.g., changes in HR policies affecting productivity and customer satisfaction).
3. **Feedback loops:**
   - **Positive feedback:** amplifies changes (e.g., viral marketing).
   - **Negative feedback:** stabilizes systems (e.g., stock level vs. reorder decisions).
4. **Non-linearity:** Outcomes are not always proportional to inputs.

Systems thinking improves strategic planning, supply chain design, risk management, and organizational learning.

1.7 The Modelling Process

A systematic modelling process ensures rigor and reliability.

1. Problem Identification

Clearly define the business issue, objectives, and constraints.

2. Model Design

Identify variables, relationships, scope, and assumptions.

3. Data Collection

Gather quantitative (sales numbers, costs) or qualitative (expert opinions) data.

4. Model Development

Construct the model using mathematical equations, diagrams, or simulation tools.

5. Testing and Validation

Check accuracy using historical data, expert validation, or sensitivity analysis.

6. Interpretation

Translate results into actionable managerial insights.

7. Implementation

Integrate model recommendations into real-world decision-making.

1.8 Managerial Skills Required for Effective Modelling

To develop, interpret, and apply models effectively, managers need:

- **Analytical thinking:** ability to break problems into components.
- **Statistical literacy:** understanding probability, trends, sampling.
- **Financial knowledge:** cash flows, costs, returns, valuation.
- **Logical reasoning:** connecting assumptions to outcomes.
- **Decision-making under uncertainty:** assessing risks and trade-offs.
- **Communication skills:** presenting results to non-technical stakeholders.

These skills ensure that modelling becomes a managerial strength rather than a technical challenge.

1.9 Applications of Modelling in Modern Business

Modelling supports almost every managerial function. Key applications include:

- **Capacity planning:** determining plant size, staffing levels, throughput.
- **Financial forecasting:** projecting revenues, expenses, cash flows.
- **Pricing decisions:** elasticity models, competitive pricing strategies.
- **Marketing analytics:** segmentation, targeting, customer lifetime value.
- **Human resource optimization:** workforce scheduling, performance assessment.
- **Supply chain coordination:** logistics, routing, inventory control.
- **Risk management:** credit risk modelling, scenario analysis.

These applications drive efficiency, innovation, and competitive advantage.

1.10 Limitations of Modelling

Despite its utility, modelling is not without challenges.

- **Simplification risks:** omitting key variables may lead to misleading conclusions.
- **Data quality issues:** inaccurate or biased data reduces validity.
- **Model overconfidence:** assuming models are perfect can lead to poor decisions.
- **Dynamic environments:** rapid external changes may invalidate static models.

- **Computational complexity:** advanced models may require skills or resources beyond managerial capacity.

Awareness of these limitations ensures responsible and cautious use of models.

1.11 Conclusion

This chapter has introduced the essential concepts, types, and significance of management and commerce modelling. By understanding modelling frameworks, systems thinking, and the modelling lifecycle, managers gain a strong foundation for advanced topics such as optimization, forecasting, simulation, strategic modelling, and data analytics. Subsequent chapters will delve deeper into specific quantitative techniques, financial models, predictive tools, and operational decision-support systems that empower modern organizations to thrive in dynamic business environments.

❐

Chapter 2

Quantitative Models for Managerial Decisions

Keywords: Linear programming, optimisation, sensitivity analysis, decision variables, constraints, simulation, statistical decision-making

Subject Classification:

- **JEL:** C61 (Optimization Techniques), D81 (Decision Theory)
- **MSC:** 90Cxx (Mathematical programming)
- **ACM CCS:** Computing methodologies → Modeling and simulation

2.1 Introduction

Quantitative models provide scientific and numerical tools to support managerial decision-making. In modern business environments—characterized by uncertainty, global competition, and large data availability—quantitative methods help managers evaluate alternatives logically, predict outcomes accurately, and choose optimal strategies. Unlike purely intuition-based decisions, quantitative models rely on measurable evidence, mathematical structures, and systematic analysis. This chapter explores core quantitative techniques that support managerial decisions, including optimization tools, statistical models, forecasting approaches, and simulation frameworks used in production planning, supply chain management, pricing, investment decisions, and risk evaluation.

2.2 Nature and Purpose of Quantitative Modelling

Quantitative modelling uses mathematical equations, numerical information, and probabilistic reasoning to represent real-world managerial problems. These models serve several purposes:

Purposes of Quantitative Models:

1. **Improve decision accuracy:** Eliminates guesswork by providing fact-based recommendations.
2. **Reduce uncertainty:** Probabilistic models help evaluate risks and expected outcomes.
3. **Optimize resource allocation:** Ensures minimal waste and maximum returns.
4. **Forecast future outcomes:** Predicts demand, revenue, costs, cash flows, etc.
5. **Evaluate alternatives:** Helps choose the best option among multiple competing strategies.

Quantitative models are most effective for problems involving numerous variables, constraints, and trade-offs—conditions typical in operations, logistics, finance, and strategic management.

2.3 Types of Quantitative Models

Quantitative models used in management fall broadly into three categories:

2.3.1 Deterministic Models

Assume all inputs are known with certainty. They do not incorporate randomness.

Examples include:

- Linear Programming (LP)
- Transportation models
- Assignment models
- Network flow models

Typical applications: production scheduling, logistics planning, staffing, manufacturing optimization.

2.3.2 Probabilistic (Stochastic) Models

Incorporate uncertainty in variables, outcomes, or parameters.

Examples:

- Decision trees
- Markov chains
- Monte Carlo simulation

Applications: risk evaluation, investment analysis, market entry planning, uncertain demand environments.

2.3.3 Statistical Predictive Models

Use historical data to forecast future behaviour.

Common types:

- Regression models
- Time-series forecasting
- Trend and seasonal decomposition

Applications: sales forecasting, cost prediction, pricing analysis, economic modelling.

2.4 Linear Programming (LP)

- Linear Programming is one of the most powerful optimization tools in management science.

2.4.1 Definition

LP is a mathematical technique used to determine the optimal allocation of limited resources to achieve a defined objective (e.g., maximize profit or minimize cost) subject to defined constraints.

2.4.2 Components of an LP Model

1. **Decision variables:** quantities the decision-maker controls.

   Example: Number of units of Product A or B to manufacture.

2. **Objective function:** a linear expression representing profit, cost, or time to be optimized.
3. **Constraints:** restrictions such as raw material availability, labor hours, machine capacity, or budget.

2.4.3 Assumptions of LP

- Linearity
- Divisibility
- Certainty
- Non-negativity

2.4.4 Business Applications

- **Production planning:** optimal product mix under resource limitations.
- **Workforce scheduling:** allocating employees to shifts.
- **Transportation & distribution:** minimizing logistics cost.
- **Portfolio optimization:** balancing risk and return.

2.5 Transportation and Assignment Models

2.5.1 Transportation Model

Optimizes the distribution of goods from multiple sources to multiple destinations at minimal cost.

Applications:

- Multi-warehouse to multi-store distribution
- Supply chain cost optimization
- Allocation of fuel, inventory, raw materials

Models consider costs, supply at origins, and demand at destinations.

2.5.2 Assignment Model

Used for one-to-one allocation problems where the aim is to minimize cost or maximize efficiency.

Examples:

- Assigning employees to tasks
- Allocating machines to jobs
- Assigning salespeople to regions
- Scheduling pilots or crew in airlines

Assignment models often use the **Hungarian Algorithm** for optimization.

2.6 Decision Trees

Decision trees provide a graphical method to analyse decisions under uncertainty.

2.6.1 Components

- **Decision nodes:** points where a manager chooses an action.

- **Chance nodes:** represent uncertain events with associated probabilities.
- **Payoffs:** profit, cost, or utility outcomes of each branch.

Why Decision Trees are Useful

- Evaluate sequential decisions
- Compute **Expected Monetary Value (EMV)**
- Compare multiple strategies under uncertainty

Example Applications

- Investment evaluation
- New product introduction
- Market entry or expansion strategy
- Risk management scenarios

Decision trees help managers visualize complex decisions and quantify risks.

2.7 Simulation Models

Simulation models mimic real-life business systems using computational methods.

2.7.1 Monte Carlo Simulation

Uses random sampling to estimate outcomes where uncertainty is high.

Common Uses:

- Project risk estimation
- Sales and revenue forecasting
- Capital budgeting under uncertainty
- Pricing and stock market scenarios

Monte Carlo models allow managers to test multiple scenarios and understand risk distributions.

2.7.2 System Dynamics Simulation

Focuses on modeling systems with feedback loops, time delays, and interconnected variables.

Applications:

- Supply chain bullwhip analysis
- Policy impact evaluation
- Market diffusion modelling (e.g., product adoption)
- Organizational growth models
- System dynamics is widely used for long-term planning and policy analysis.

2.8 Statistical Models for Managerial Decisions

Statistical techniques help managers analyse data and uncover insights.

2.8.1 Regression Analysis

Explores relationships between dependent and independent variables.

Applications:

- Predicting sales from advertising expenditure
- Estimating cost from production volume
- Forecasting profitability from market factors

Regression is foundational for analytics and decision science.

2.8.2 Correlation Analysis

Measures the strength and direction of relationships between variables.

Used to:

- Identify key performance drivers
- Detect multicollinearity in models
- Analyse customer behaviour patterns

2.8.3 Time-Series Forecasting

Analyses data over time to identify trends, cycles, and seasonality.

Methods include:

- Moving averages
- Exponential smoothing
- ARIMA models

Applications:

- Sales demand forecasting
- Inventory planning
- Budget estimation
- Financial projections
- Time-series models help firms anticipate future requirements and manage resources proactively.

2.9 Cost–Volume–Profit (CVP) Analysis

Cost–Volume–Profit analysis examines the relationship among cost structures, sales volume, and profit.

Key Components:

- **Contribution margin**
- **Break-even point**
- **Margin of safety**
- **Operating leverage**

Managerial Uses:

- Pricing decisions
- Profit planning
- Product mix evaluation
- Capacity planning

CVP helps business leaders understand how changes in cost or volume affect profitability.

2.10 Demand and Supply Modelling in Commerce

Quantitative modelling also extends to market analysis.

Demand Models

Estimate how price, income, and other factors influence quantity demanded.

Used for:

- Pricing strategy
- Revenue management
- Market forecasting

Supply Models

Analyse production costs, capacity, and constraints affecting quantity supplied.

Useful in:

- Production planning
- Procurement decisions
- Capacity expansion

Combined models support competitive strategy and market equilibrium analysis.

2.11 Case Illustrations

Case 1: Production Planning using LP

A manufacturing firm produces two products with limited labor and raw material. LP helps determine the product mix that maximizes profit.

Case 2: Pricing Decision using Regression

A retail company analyses historical sales and advertising data to determine optimal pricing strategies.

Case 3: Inventory Planning using Forecasting

A logistics company uses ARIMA models to forecast seasonal demand and optimize inventory levels.

Case 4: Market Entry Decision using Decision Trees

A firm evaluates different market expansion strategies considering probabilities of success and potential revenues.

2.12 Conclusion

Quantitative models form the backbone of modern managerial decision-making. Whether optimizing production, forecasting demand, evaluating risks, or designing pricing strategies, these models provide rigorous frameworks that reduce uncertainty and support rational decision-making. As businesses continue to embrace analytics and data science, mastery of quantitative modelling becomes an essential competency for future managers.

❑

Chapter 3

Financial & Economic Modelling

3.1 Introduction

Financial and economic modelling provides systematic, quantitative frameworks for analysing business performance, evaluating investment opportunities, forecasting future trends, and understanding interactions within markets and economies. In an increasingly data-driven world, managers, policymakers, and financial analysts rely on modelling techniques to make informed and evidence-based decisions. Financial models capture firm- or investor-level behaviour—such as profitability, capital structure, and cash flows—while economic models explain aggregate phenomena including inflation, GDP growth, unemployment, interest rates, and consumption dynamics. Together, these models create a holistic understanding of both micro-level decisions and macro-level outcomes. This chapter introduces foundational principles, methodologies, and applications of financial and economic modelling, with emphasis on decision-making under uncertainty, risk evaluation, and strategic planning.

3.2 Fundamentals of Financial Modelling

3.2.1 Definition and Purpose

Financial modelling refers to constructing mathematical and logical representations of real-world financial scenarios. A financial model enables users to:

- Estimate firm or asset valuation
- Predict future revenues, expenses, and cash flows
- Assess investment feasibility (capital budgeting)
- Analyse financial risks and uncertainties
- Evaluate financing options and capital structure
- Optimise risk–return trade-offs
- Support strategic decision-making through scenarios and forecasting

These models serve purposes ranging from internal budgeting to equity valuation, mergers and acquisitions, and policy analysis.

3.2.2 Structure of a Financial Model

A robust financial model typically contains:

1. **Input Assumptions**
    - Revenue drivers (price, quantity, market size)
    - Cost structures (fixed vs. variable)
    - Growth assumptions
    - Tax rates, inflation, discount rates
    - Working capital adjustments
2. **Processing Components**
    - Logical formulas, financial equations
    - Accounting relationships
    - Algorithms for forecasting, depreciation, amortization
    - Scenario and risk modules
3. **Outputs**
    - Projected financial statements (income statement, balance sheet, cash flow)

- Key financial ratios (Liquidity, profitability, leverage)
- Valuation metrics (NPV, IRR, EVA, WACC)
- Sensitivity/Scenario reports

A good model is transparent, flexible, auditable, and reliable.

3.2.3 Types of Financial Models

1. Discounted Cash Flow (DCF) Model

Evaluates firm or project value based on discounted free cash flows. Widely used for equity valuation.

2. Three-Statement Model

Integrates income statement, balance sheet, and cash flow statement, linking all assumptions dynamically.

3. Capital Budgeting Models

Used to assess investment feasibility:

- Net Present Value (NPV)
- Internal Rate of Return (IRR)
- Payback Period
- Profitability Index (PI)

4. Risk and Portfolio Models

- Capital Asset Pricing Model (CAPM)
- Efficient Frontier (Markowitz)
- Beta estimation
- Value-at-Risk (VaR)
- Useful in portfolio construction and risk management.

5. Leveraged Buyout (LBO) Models

Assess acquisition viability when financed mostly through debt. Key focus: debt repayment and investor return.

6. Forecasting Models

Based on regression, time-series, neural networks, and machine learning for revenue or market prediction.

3.3 Core Tools of Financial Modelling

3.3.1 Time Value of Money (TVM)

TVM recognizes that **money today is worth more than money tomorrow** due to investment opportunities and inflation.

Key concepts:

- Present Value (PV)
- Future Value (FV)
- Discount rate (r)
- Number of periods (n)
- Compounding (annual, quarterly, continuous)

Formula:

$$PV = FV(1+r)^n$$

Real applications:

- Loan amortization
- Retirement planning
- Bond valuation
- Capital budgeting

3.3.2 Cost of Capital

Cost of capital reflects the required return demanded by investors.

Weighted Average Cost of Capital (WACC):

$$WACC = EVke + DVkd(1 - T)$$

Where:

- E = Equity
- D = Debt
- V = E + D = Firm value

Cost of Equity (CAPM):

$$E(Ri) = Rf + \beta i(Rm - Rf)$$

Cost of Debt:

Interest expense adjusted for tax benefits.

3.3.3 Financial Ratios and Performance Metrics

1. **Liquidity ratios** – Current ratio, Quick ratio
2. **Profitability ratios** – ROA, ROE, Gross/Net Profit Margin
3. **Efficiency ratios** – Asset turnover, Inventory turnover
4. **Leverage ratios** – Debt-equity, Interest-coverage
5. **Market ratios** – P/E, P/BV, Dividend yield

Models often forecast these ratios to assess business health over time.

3.3.4 Risk Modelling

Risk modelling quantifies uncertainty in financial outcomes.

Tools include:

- **Variance & Standard Deviation** (volatility)
- **Covariance & Correlation** (asset co-movement)
- **Portfolio Optimization** (minimum variance portfolio)
- **Monte Carlo Simulation** – randomised scenarios for thousands of outcomes

Applications:

Stock valuation • Option pricing • Project risk assessment • Credit risk models

3.4 Economic Modelling: Concepts & Scope

3.4.1 Definition

Economic modelling constructs quantitative representations of economic structures to:

- Predict macroeconomic trends
- Understand consumer/firm behaviour
- Evaluate economic policies
- Study general equilibrium and market interactions

3.4.2 Types of Economic Models

1. **Microeconomic Models**
    - Consumer utility maximization
    - Firm production functions (Cobb-Douglas)
    - Market equilibrium
2. **Macroeconomic Models**
    - IS–LM (interest–income equilibrium)
    - AD–AS (inflation-output relationship)
    - Solow Growth Model
    - Business cycle models
3. **Econometric Models**
    - Regression-based forecasting (inflation, GDP)
4. **CGE Models (Computable General Equilibrium)**

Used for trade policy, taxation reforms, climate policy.

5. **Input–Output Models**

Explore inter-industry linkages and structural changes.

3.4.3 Key Components

- **Endogenous variables** – output, consumption, inflation
- **Exogenous variables** – policy rates, technological change
- **Behavioural equations** – consumption, investment
- **Equilibrium conditions** – market-clearing
- **Constraints** – budget, policy, resource limits

3.5 Econometric and Statistical Foundations

3.5.1 Regression Analysis

Regression establishes statistical relationships:

$$Y = \beta 0 + \beta 1\ X1 + \ldots + \beta n\ Xn + \epsilon$$

Applications:

- Demand estimation
- Revenue forecasting
- Price prediction
- Economic indicator modelling

3.5.2 Time-Series Modelling

Used for forecasting variables over time.

Models:

- **AR (Auto-Regressive)**
- **MA (Moving Average)**
- **ARIMA**

- **Seasonal ARIMA**
- **Vector Auto-Regressive (VAR)** for multi-variable systems

Concepts:

- Trend
- Seasonality
- Stationarity
- Unit root tests (ADF, PP)

3.5.3 Panel Data Models

Combine time-series and cross-sectional data.

- **Fixed Effects (FE)** – controls for time-invariant traits
- **Random Effects (RE)** – assumes random variation
- **Difference-in-Difference (DiD)** – used in policy impact evaluation

3.6 Financial–Economic Integration

3.6.1 Linking Micro & Macro Perspectives

Examples:

- Interest rate hike → higher discount rate → lower firm valuation
- Exchange rate volatility → affects exporters' profitability
- Inflation → increases cost structure → affects pricing decisions

3.6.2 Business Cycle and Financial Markets

Models examine:

- Pro-cyclical industries (luxury goods, real estate)
- Counter-cyclical industries (FMCG, healthcare)

- Asset pricing during recessions
- Stress testing under shocks (oil price surge, global crisis)

3.6.3 Corporate Strategy Under Economic Uncertainty

- Hedging currency, interest rate risk
- Dynamic capital structure adjustment
- Forecasting demand across business cycles
- Using real options for strategic investment timing

3.7 Applications of Financial & Economic Modelling

3.7.1 Investment Analysis

- Equity valuation (DCF, multiples)
- Bond valuation and yield modelling
- Portfolio construction and optimization
- Start-up valuation (venture capital methods)
- Real options for strategic flexibility

3.7.2 Corporate Financial Planning

- Budgeting
- Forecasting
- Working capital modelling
- Dividend policy planning
- Cost-volume-profit (CVP) analysis

3.7.3 Market & Policy Analysis

- Inflation forecasting for pricing
- Exchange-rate models for multinational strategy
- Government policy impact assessments (CGE, I-O models)

3.7.4 Industry-Specific Models

- **Banking** – Credit scoring, default probability
- **Insurance** – Actuarial models
- **Energy** – Commodity price models, demand forecasting
- **Logistics** – Route cost optimization, demand modelling

3.8 Managerial Decision-Making With Modelling

3.8.1 Model-Based Decision Framework

Managers use models to:

- Compare alternatives
- Quantify costs and benefits
- Predict uncertain outcomes
- Allocate limited resources efficiently
- Measure risk exposures

3.8.2 Scenario & Sensitivity Analysis

- What-if modeling
- Tornado diagrams
- Monte Carlo simulation
- Stress tests for extreme events (e.g., recession)

3.8.3 Behavioural Aspects

Human biases affect modelling decisions:

- Overconfidence
- Anchoring bias
- Confirmation bias
- Herd behaviour

- Loss aversion
- Behavioural finance helps in interpreting irrational market patterns.

3.9 Limitations, Assumptions & Ethical Issues

3.9.1 Limitations

- Models simplify reality
- Assumptions may be unrealistic
- Sensitive to input errors
- Market behaviour often irrational
- Time-series data may face structural breaks
- Black-swan events (pandemics, wars) disrupt forecasts

3.9.2 Ethical Concerns

- Manipulation of assumptions
- Lack of transparency
- Misuse in policymaking
- Biased forecasting
- Ethical responsibility toward stakeholders

3.10 Summary

Financial and economic modelling is a critical tool in business strategy, investment analysis, and policy decision-making. Through mathematical representations, models help organisations evaluate opportunities, assess risk, and forecast future outcomes. When combined with economic insights, they support robust decision-making in complex and uncertain environments. However, their effectiveness depends on sound assumptions, reliable data, and ethical usage.

❐

Chapter 4

Statistical & Predictive Modelling for Commerce

Keywords: Regression models, forecasting, ARIMA, exponential smoothing, customer analytics, sales modelling, inventory prediction

Subject Classification:

- **JEL:** C53 (Forecasting Models), M31 (Marketing Analytics)
- **MSC:** 62Jxx (Regression Analysis), 62M10 (Time Series)
- **ACM CCS:** Information Systems → Data Analytics

4.0 Introduction

Statistical and predictive modelling forms the analytical foundation of modern commerce. With increasing availability of data from digital transactions, customer interactions, and supply chain networks, businesses rely heavily on quantitative methods to detect patterns, forecast future behaviour, and optimise operations. This chapter discusses essential statistical tools used in commerce, including regression analysis, time-series forecasting, customer behaviour modelling, retail sales prediction, and inventory/logistics forecasting. These models support decision-making across marketing, finance, operations, supply chain management, e-commerce, and retail environments.

4.1 Regression Models

Regression models quantify relationships between business variables and help explain, predict, and optimize outcomes. They are central to marketing analytics, sales forecasting, customer modelling, financial analysis, and operational planning.

4.1.1 Simple Linear Regression

Simple linear regression models the linear relationship between a dependent variable and one independent variable:

$$Y = \beta 0 + \beta 1X + \epsilon$$

Where:

- Y: response variable (sales, revenue)
- X: predictor variable (price, advertising spend)
- β0, β1 : coefficients
- ϵ: error term

Applications:

- Predicting monthly *sales* from advertising expenditure
- Estimating *labour cost* from output volume
- Determining the *price–demand* relationship

4.1.2 Multiple Regression

Many business outcomes depend on multiple factors. Multiple regression expands the model:

$$Y = \beta 0 + \beta 1\ X1 + \beta 2\ X2 + \cdots + \beta k\ Xk + \epsilon$$

Applications in Commerce:

- Sales forecasting using price + promotion + seasonality + competitor pricing
- Profit estimation using labour, raw materials, and overhead

- Customer satisfaction modelling from service quality indicators

Advantages:

- Incorporates complex relationships
- Identifies key influencers (elasticities, sensitivities)
- Enables scenario testing ("What happens if price increases by 5%?")

4.1.3 Logistic Regression

Used when the outcome is binary (purchase/no purchase, churn/stay, default/no default).

$$P(Y = 1) = e^{\beta 0} + \beta 1\ X1 + \cdots$$

Applications:

- Churn prediction in telecom, banking, SaaS
- Predicting probability of loan default
- Estimating likelihood of response to email/ advertisements
- Classification of high-value vs. low-value customers

4.2 Forecasting Techniques

Forecasting is essential for budgeting, resource allocation, pricing, staffing, and inventory management. Time-series forecasting uses historical patterns—including trend, seasonality, and cycles—to predict future behaviour.

4.2.1 ARIMA Models (Auto-Regressive Integrated Moving Average)

ARIMA is one of the most widely used statistical forecasting models.

General form: **ARIMA(p, d, q)**

- p: autoregressive component
- d: differencing order to remove trend
- q: moving average component

Steps in ARIMA modelling:

1. Identify stationarity (ADF/PP test)
2. Apply differencing if needed
3. Select model order using AIC/BIC
4. Fit ARIMA model
5. Validate using residual diagnostics

Applications:

- Retail sales forecasting
- Supply and demand planning
- Financial and commodity price forecasting
- Forecasting electricity demand or airline passengers

4.2.2 Exponential Smoothing Models

These models apply decaying weights to past observations.

(a) Simple Exponential Smoothing (SES)

For series with no trend or seasonality.

Forecast equation:

$$F_{t+1} = \alpha Y_t + (1-\alpha)F_t$$

(b) Holt's Linear Trend Method

Captures level + trend components.

(c) Holt–Winters Method

Used for seasonal data (additive or multiplicative seasonality).

Applications:

- Seasonal retail product forecasts (e.g., festival sales)
- Workforce planning and labour scheduling
- Inventory demand smoothing
- Short-term operational forecasting

4.3 Customer Behaviour Modelling

Predicting customer actions is central to marketing strategy, CRM, product recommendations, and retention planning.

4.3.1 RFM Analysis (Recency, Frequency, Monetary Value)

Customers are segmented by:

- **Recency** – last purchase date
- **Frequency** – number of purchases
- **Monetary Value** – total amount spent

Uses:

- Targeted digital marketing
- Loyalty and rewards program design
- Identifying high-value customer segments
- Reducing marketing costs through segmentation

4.3.2 Customer Lifetime Value (CLV)

CLV predicts the future profit a business can expect from a customer over their relationship lifespan.

CLV=∑t=1T(Revenue_t−Cost_t)(1+r)t

CLV=\sum_{t=1}^{T}\frac{(Revenue_t - Cost_t)}{(1+r)^t}

CLV=t=1∑T(1+r)t(Revenue_t−Cost_t)

Uses:

- Budgeting customer acquisition cost
- Setting optimal pricing strategies
- Identifying profitable vs. unprofitable customers
- Designing retention and engagement policies

4.3.3 Churn Prediction Models

Uses machine learning or regression to identify customers likely to stop using a service.

Techniques:

- Logistic regression
- Decision trees & Random Forest
- Gradient boosting (XGBoost)
- Survival analysis

Applications:

- Telecom, banking, insurance retention
- Subscription-based services (OTT, SaaS)
- Proactive customer support interventions

4.4 Retail Sales Modelling

Retail is highly data-driven, making predictive modelling essential for merchandising, pricing, promotions, and store operations.

4.4.1 Price–Demand Modelling

Explores demand elasticity to price.

Techniques:

- Linear or log-linear regression
- Elasticity models
- Econometric models (e.g., log-log demand function)

Applications:

- Optimal pricing
- Discount planning
- Revenue optimization

4.4.2 Market Basket Analysis

Identifies product co-purchase patterns.

Most common method: **Apriori algorithm**

Example:

- Customers buying *tea* often buy *sugar*.
- "Buy 1, get 1 free" combinations
- Cross-selling on e-commerce platforms

Applications:

- Product bundling
- Store layout optimisation
- Recommendation systems

4.4.3 Sales Forecasting Using Time-Series Models

Techniques:

- ARIMA
- Holt-Winters
- Regression with seasonality
- Machine learning models:
    - Random Forest
    - XGBoost
    - LSTM neural networks

Uses:

- Holiday and festival demand prediction
- Marketing budget allocation
- Workforce scheduling
- Inventory and supply planning

4.5 Inventory and Logistics Forecasting

Predictive models enable companies to maintain the right amount of inventory, reduce stockouts, and streamline logistics.

4.5.1 Inventory Demand Forecasting

Key factors:

- Historical demand
- Lead time
- Supplier reliability
- Seasonality
- Promotional effects

Common techniques:

- EOQ (Economic Order Quantity)
- Safety stock calculation
- ARIMA/Exponential smoothing for demand
- Machine learning models

4.5.2 Supply Chain Predictive Models

Forecasts:

- Delivery time variability
- Transportation cost
- Warehouse processing delays
- Bottleneck identification

Techniques:

- Regression models
- Time-series models
- Simulation models
- Network optimisation algorithms

4.5.3 ABC Analysis

Categorizes inventory:

- **A items:** high value, low volume → tight control
- **B items:** moderate value and demand
- **C items:** low value, high volume → simpler controls

Applications:

- Purchase planning
- Warehouse slotting
- Resource allocation

Conclusion

Statistical and predictive modelling equips commerce professionals with quantitative tools to analyse patterns, forecast future outcomes, and optimize business decisions. From regression techniques to advanced forecasting models and customer analytics, these tools enhance operational efficiency, reduce risk, and strengthen competitiveness. Mastery of these models allows businesses to anticipate trends, improve customer satisfaction, and achieve sustainable profitability.

❐

Chapter 5
Computational Modelling & Decision Support Systems

Keywords: Monte Carlo simulation, system dynamics, decision trees, scenario modelling, DSS, expert systems, optimisation algorithms

Subject Classification:

- **JEL:** C63 (Computational Techniques), C44 (Decision Support Systems)
- **MSC:** 68T30 (Knowledge representation), 91A80 (Decision theory)
- **ACM CCS:** Artificial Intelligence → Decision Support Systems

5.0 Introduction

Computational modelling and Decision Support Systems (DSS) form the backbone of analytical decision-making in modern organizations. As environments grow in complexity—due to globalization, technological change, volatile markets, and uncertain demand—traditional intuition-driven decisions are insufficient. Computational models provide the ability to:

- Examine multiple alternatives
- Simulate uncertain environments
- Predict outcomes of complex decisions

- Optimize resource allocation
- Embed expert reasoning into automated systems

This chapter introduces simulation tools (Monte Carlo and system dynamics), structured decision techniques (decision trees and scenarios), multi-criteria decision analysis (MCDA), and intelligent systems (expert systems and DSS frameworks).

5.1 Simulation Modelling

Simulation modelling recreates real-world processes inside a computational environment. It is especially useful when experimentation in real systems is expensive, slow, risky, or impossible.

5.1.1 Monte Carlo Simulation

Monte Carlo simulation uses repeated random sampling to compute results for uncertain problems.

Key Characteristics

- Treats inputs as **probability distributions** (Normal, Triangular, Poisson, etc.)
- Runs **thousands of simulations** to approximate the distribution of outcomes
- Generates **risk profiles**, not just point estimates
- Supports **sensitivity analysis** to identify critical drivers

Common Applications

- **Finance:** Value at Risk (VaR), asset pricing, option valuation
- **Operations:** Inventory uncertainty, lead-time simulation
- **Marketing:** Demand forecasting with uncertain response

- **Project Management:** PERT/CPM with probabilistic task durations
- **Pricing:** Revenue risk analysis under uncertain elasticity

Illustrative Examples

A company simulates **monthly profit** using probability distributions for:

- Demand (Normal distribution)
- Price elasticity (Triangular distribution)
- Competitor action probability
- Cost variation

Running 10,000 simulations yields:

- Mean profit
- Probability of loss
- Best- and worst-case scenarios
- Confidence intervals

This enables risk-aware strategic decisions.

5.1.2 System Dynamics

System Dynamics (SD), developed by Jay Forrester, models complex systems with interacting feedback loops, delays, and accumulations.

Core Components

- **Stocks:** quantities that accumulate (inventory, population, capacity)
- **Flows:** rates of change (production rate, hiring rate)
- **Feedback loops:** reinforcing (positive) or balancing (negative)

- **Delays:** time lags that create oscillations and instability

Modelling Capabilities

SD excels at modelling systems exhibiting:

- Exponential growth or decay
- Oscillation cycles
- Nonlinear behaviour
- Long-term policy impacts

Applications

- Supply chain bullwhip effect **modelling**
- Economic policy simulation
- Human resource capacity planning
- Sustainability and ecological modelling
- Project dynamics & rework cycles

Value of SD

Managers gain insights into:

- Why systems behave unexpectedly
- How short-term decisions create long-term consequences
- Hidden interdependencies and leverage points

5.2 Decision Trees & Scenario Modelling

5.2.1 Decision Trees

Decision trees are graphical decision tools that map sequential decisions under uncertainty.

Components

- **Decision nodes (□)**: choices
- **Chance nodes (○)**: uncertain events with probabilities

- **Terminal nodes (Δ)**: payoffs

Advantages

- Easy visual interpretation
- Supports **expected value** and **risk analysis**
- Handles sequential or multi-stage decisions
- Useful for investment decisions, R&D choices, policy evaluation

Example Use Cases

- Whether to expand a factory under uncertain demand
- Product launch decisions with market acceptance probabilities
- Choose between outsourcing vs. in-house production

5.2.2 Scenario Modelling

Scenario modelling explores alternative future states to prepare organizations for uncertainty.

Types of Scenarios

- **Best-case**
- **Worst-case**
- **Most likely**
- **Extreme shocks** (policy change, recession, supply disruptions)
- **Technology disruption scenarios**

Applications

- Market entry viability
- Long-term capacity planning

- Strategic risk management
- Capital budgeting
- Revenue forecasting under macroeconomic shocks

Scenario modelling is often paired with simulation or optimisation for deeper insights.

5.3 Multi-Criteria Decision Analysis (MCDA)

Real decisions involve trade-offs across conflicting criteria such as cost, quality, risk, sustainability, and customer satisfaction.

MCDA provides tools to evaluate alternatives considering multiple dimensions.

5.3.1 MCDA Techniques

1. **Weighted Scoring Model (WSM)**

Total Score = ∑(wi×si)\text{Total Score} = \sum (w_i\times s_i)Total Score = ∑(wi×si)

2. **Analytic Hierarchy Process (AHP)**
    - Uses pairwise comparisons
    - Computes priority weights
    - Includes **consistency ratio** to validate judgments

AHP is widely used for strategic decisions with both quantitative and qualitative factors.

3. **TOPSIS (Technique for Order Preference by Similarity to Ideal Solution)**
    - Identifies alternatives closest to the ideal solution
    - Used heavily in supplier ranking, project evaluation, and financial decision-making

MCDA Applications

- Vendor/supplier selection
- Capital investment decisions
- New product evaluation
- Facility location selection
- Public policy design

5.4 Expert Systems & Decision Support Tools

5.4.1 Expert Systems

Expert systems mimic human expert reasoning using:

- **Knowledge base:** rules, facts, heuristics
- **Inference engine:** applies logic
- **User interface:** interacts with the decision-maker

Applications

- Medical diagnosis
- Loan approval and fraud detection
- Technical troubleshooting
- Customer support automation
- Legal reasoning

5.4.2 Decision Support Systems (DSS)

DSS integrates data, analytical models, and domain knowledge.

Types of DSS

1. **Data-driven DSS:** BI dashboards, OLAP, data warehouses
2. **Model-driven DSS:** optimization, forecasting, simulation

3. **Knowledge-driven DSS:** expert systems, AI-enabled advisors
4. **Communication-driven DSS:** group decision tools

Benefits

- Improved accuracy
- Faster decisions
- Transparency and auditability
- Enhanced strategic planning
- What-if and sensitivity analysis

Conclusion

Computational modelling and DSS empower managers with data-driven, structured, and intelligent tools. They provide the capability to simulate uncertainty, evaluate complex decisions, integrate expert knowledge, and optimize strategic choices in dynamic environments.

❒

Chapter 6
Modelling in Marketing & Consumer Analytics**

Keywords: Consumer segmentation, CLV, market response, digital marketing analytics, social media modeling.

Subject Classification:

- **JEL:** M31 (Marketing), C55 (Large Data Modelling)
- **MSC:** 91B42 (Consumer Behavior), 68T05 (Data Mining)
- **ACM CCS:** Applied Computing → Marketing

6.0 Introduction

Marketing has transformed into a data-intensive discipline powered by computational models, machine learning, behavioural psychology, and digital analytics. Modern marketing decisions depend on consumer insights extracted through segmentation, customer value modelling, market response estimation, and digital behaviour analysis. This chapter explores the analytical frameworks essential to marketing strategy and customer-centric decision-making.

6.1 Consumer Segmentation Models

Segmentation divides a heterogeneous market into meaningful, homogeneous consumer groups.

6.1.1 Segmentation Types

1. Demographic

Age, gender, education, income, occupation

2. Psychographic

Personality, lifestyle, values, interests

3. Behavioural

Usage frequency, loyalty, recency, channel preference

4. Geographic

City size, climate, density, region

6.1.2 Statistical Segmentation Models

Cluster Analysis

- K-means
- Hierarchical clustering
- Gaussian Mixture Models

Latent Class Models

Probabilistic classification uncovering hidden behavioural segments.

RFM Segmentation

Scores customers based on:

- Recency
- Frequency
- Monetary value

Used in retail, e-commerce, and loyalty programmes.

6.2 Customer Lifetime Value (CLV) Modelling

CLV estimates long-term profitability of customers and guides resource allocation.

6.2.1 Deterministic CLV Model

CLV = ∑t = 1TRt−Ct(1+r)t

CLV = \sum_{t=1}^{T}\frac{R_t - C_t}{(1+r)^t}

CLV = t = 1∑T(1+r)tRt−Ct

6.2.2 Probabilistic CLV Models

BG/NBD Model

Predicts customer purchase frequency and churn probability.

Pareto/NBD Model

Used for contractual and non-contractual settings.

Gamma–Gamma Model

Estimates customer spending amount.

6.2.3 CLV Applications

- Optimizing acquisition spending
- Identifying high-value customers
- Loyalty programme design
- Predictive churn management
- Personalization & recommendation systems

6.3 Market Response Models

These models measure the effect of marketing actions on demand.

6.3.1 Regression-Based Demand Models

$$Sales = \beta 0 + \beta 1 Price + \beta 2 Advertising + \beta 3 Promotion + \epsilon$$

Uses: demand estimation, pricing strategy, ROI measurement.

6.3.2 Marketing Mix Models (MMM)

Quantifies channel contributions to sales using:

- Advertising
- Trade promotions
- Online channels
- Price dynamics
- Seasonality

Outputs include:

- Base vs. incremental sales
- Diminishing returns
- Channel ROI
- Optimal budget allocation

6.3.3 Diffusion Models

Bass Diffusion Model

Predicts adoption pattern of new products with:

- **p:** innovation
- **q:** imitation

Used for forecasting consumer durables, apps, technology products.

6.4 Digital Marketing Analytics Models

Digital channels provide granular behavioural data for advanced modelling.

6.4.1 Attribution Modelling

- First-touch
- Last-touch
- Linear
- Time decay
- Algorithmic attribution

6.4.2 Web & App Analytics

Measures include:

- CTR, CR
- Bounce rate
- Funnel drop-off
- Session duration
- Heatmaps

6.4.3 Predictive Digital Models

Uses machine learning for:

- Click prediction
- Lead scoring
- Customer churn
- Personalization
- Campaign optimization

6.5 Social Media Influence Modelling

6.5.1 Social Network Analysis (SNA)

Key metrics:

- Degree centrality
- Betweenness centrality

- Community detection
- Eigenvector centrality

Applications:

- Opinion leader identification
- Viral marketing design
- Influence mapping

6.5.2 Sentiment Analysis

Uses NLP to extract sentiment from text.

Applications:

- Brand monitoring
- Customer feedback mining
- Crisis management

6.5.3 Influence Propagation Models

- Independent Cascade Model
- Linear Threshold Model

Used for viral campaigns, trend prediction, and information diffusion.

Conclusion

Marketing and consumer analytics provide powerful data-driven methodologies for understanding customer needs, predicting behaviour, and optimizing marketing investments.

❒

Chapter 7

Operations & Supply Chain Modelling

Keywords: EOQ, MRP, logistics routing, VRP, Lean, Six Sigma, supply chain optimisation

Subject Classification: JEL L23, R40 | MSC 90B06, 90B05 | ACM OR Systems

7.0 Introduction

Operations and supply chain modelling ensures efficient operations, optimized logistics, cost reduction, and service excellence. These models help organizations handle global supply chains, uncertain demand, complex routing, and quality improvement.

7.1 Supply Chain Network Design

Decisions include:

- Number/location of facilities
- Sourcing strategy
- Capacity allocation
- Product flows

7.1.1 Strategic Network Design

Objectives:

- Minimize costs
- Maximize service levels
- Ensure resilience

7.1.2 Mathematical Formulation

Minimize Total Cost = Facility + Transport + Production

Constraints:

- Capacity limits
- Demand satisfaction
- Feasibility & routing constraints

Techniques: LP, MIP, Heuristics, Met heuristics.

7.1.3 Applications

- E-commerce fulfillment design
- Global sourcing strategy
- Multi-echelon supply chains

7.2 Inventory & Warehouse Modelling

7.2.1 EOQ

EOQ = $[2DSH]^{0.5}$

7.2.2 ABC Analysis

Classifies inventory by value contribution.

7.2.3 MRP System

Inputs:

- MPS
- BOM
- Inventory records

Outputs:

- Planned order releases
- Purchase orders

7.2.4 Warehouse Modelling

Includes:

- Slotting optimization
- Picking route algorithms
- Layout optimization
- Simulation models

7.3 Logistics Routing Models

7.3.1 VRP Variants

- CVRP
- VRPTW
- Stochastic VRP
- Dynamic VRP

Solutions via heuristics, metaheuristics, or exact MIP.

7.3.2 Last-Mile Delivery

Models include:

- Drone routing
- Crowdsourcing logistics
- Density optimization

7.3.3 Transportation Network Optimization

Used for multi-modal planning and freight routing.

7.4 Lean & Six Sigma Models

7.4.1 Lean Tools

- VSM
- Kaizen

- 5S
- Little's Law:

$$WIP = \lambda TWIP = \backslash lambda\ TWIP = \lambda T$$

7.4.2 Six Sigma Tools

- Control charts
- DOE
- Capability indices (Cp, Cpk)
- Root cause analysis

Conclusion

Operations and supply chain models support efficiency, resilience, and cost minimization across global supply chains.

❒

Chapter 8

Human Resource & Organizational Behaviour Modelling

Keywords: workforce planning, ONA, competency modelling, climate, culture

Subject Classification: JEL M50, D91 | MSC 91Bxx | ACM Enterprise Modelling

8.0 Introduction

HR and OB analytics combine behavioural science, statistics, and computational analytics to improve workforce strategy and organizational effectiveness.

8.1 Workforce Planning Models

8.1.1 Demand Forecasting

- Trend models
- Regression models
- Ratio analysis
- Workload-based manpower calculation

8.1.2 Supply Forecasting

- Attrition probabilities
- Promotion rates
- Retirement models
- Markov chain forecasting

8.1.3 Gap Analysis

- Staffing shortages
- Training requirements
- Automation vs. hiring decisions

8.2 Competency & Productivity Modelling

8.2.1 Competency Mapping

Tools:

- 360 feedback
- BEI
- Skill matrices
- Job analysis

8.2.2 Productivity Models

- KPI, OKR modelling
- DEA (efficiency frontier)
- Time series productivity analysis
- Balanced scorecard integration

Key drivers:

- Skills
- Motivation
- Technology
- Work environment

8.3 Behavioural Modelling Using Surveys

8.3.1 HR/OB Surveys

- Job satisfaction
- Engagement
- Leadership
- Stress & well-being

8.3.2 Statistical Modelling

- Descriptive analysis
- Factor analysis
- Reliability testing
- SEM (structural equation modelling)

8.4 Organizational Network Analysis (ONA)

Maps informal networks.

Metrics:

- Centrality
- Betweenness
- Density
- Modularity

Used for:

- Identifying influencers
- Diagnosing silos
- Communication flow analysis

8.5 Climate & Culture Modelling

8.5.1 Climate

Measured using:

- Surveys
- Climate strength modelling
- Multilevel analysis

8.5.2 Culture

Models:

- Schein

- CVF
- OCAI

Used for:

- Transformation initiatives
- Leadership development
- Integration after mergers

Conclusion

HR and OB modelling equips organizations with analytical insights to improve workforce capability, cultural health, and organizational performance.

❐

Chapter 9

Strategic Management Modelling

Keywords: Strategy maps, Balanced Scorecard, competitive forces, industry analysis, scenario planning, transformation models.

Subject Classification:

- **JEL:** M10 (Business Strategy), L10 (Market Structure)
- **MSC:** 91B74 (Decision Sciences), 68U35 (Business Modelling)
- **ACM CCS:** Applied computing → Strategic management systems

Strategic management modelling plays a crucial role in enabling organizations to analyze competitive environments, establish long-term goals, evaluate strategic options, and monitor performance. In an increasingly volatile and dynamic global environment, modelling frameworks offer structured and quantitative approaches to decision-making, ensuring alignment between strategy, operations, and organizational capabilities. This chapter explores key analytical and modelling tools that support strategic planning and execution, including strategy maps, the Balanced Scorecard, competitive and industry models, business transformation models, and scenario planning methodologies.

9.1 Strategy Maps & Balanced Scorecard

9.1.1 Concept of Strategy Maps

A **strategy map** is a visual representation that illustrates how an organization creates value through interconnected strategic objectives. Typically built on the Balanced Scorecard architecture, a strategy map shows cause-and-effect linkages between intangible assets (knowledge, innovation, leadership) and tangible outcomes (profitability, market share, competitive advantage).

Key characteristics:

- Clear cause-and-effect relationships
- Alignment of strategic objectives
- Integration of people, processes, and technology
- Transparency in strategy communication
- Support for cross-functional alignment

Strategy maps provide clarity to stakeholders and serve as a communication tool for explaining how strategic goals translate into operational initiatives.

9.1.2 Balanced Scorecard (BSC)

Developed by **Kaplan and Norton**, the Balanced Scorecard is both a performance measurement system and a strategic management framework. It emphasizes a balanced approach by examining an organization from four interconnected perspectives:

1. Financial Perspective

- Profitability
- Return on Investment (ROI)
- Cost efficiency
- Shareholder value

2. Customer Perspective

- Customer satisfaction
- Retention and loyalty
- Market share
- Value propositions

3. Internal Process Perspective

- Quality management
- Innovation processes
- Operational efficiency
- Supply chain and logistics

4. Learning & Growth Perspective

- Employee skills
- Leadership and culture
- Technology infrastructure
- Knowledge management

The BSC helps organizations move beyond purely financial metrics toward a holistic understanding of performance drivers.

9.1.3 Modelling with the BSC

The Balanced Scorecard enables organizations to:

- Convert strategy into measurable objectives
- Develop relevant performance indicators (KPIs)
- Align operational activities with strategic targets
- Use real-time dashboards for decision support
- Monitor performance trends and adapt strategies

Modelling practices include:

- Assigning weights to perspectives and objectives
- Constructing composite scorecard indices
- Using Multi-Criteria Decision-Making tools (AHP, TOPSIS)
- Applying predictive analytics to forecast KPI outcomes

These modelling techniques support strategic prioritization and continuous performance improvement.

9.2 Competitive Forces and Industry Modelling

9.2.1 Porter's Five Forces Model

Porter's Five Forces framework evaluates the competitive intensity of an industry. The five forces include:

1. Industry Rivalry
2. Threat of New Entrants
3. Threat of Substitutes
4. Bargaining Power of Suppliers
5. Bargaining Power of Buyers

This analysis helps determine industry attractiveness, structural profitability, and strategic positioning options.

9.2.2 Strategic Modelling Techniques

Industry and competitive analysis frequently employ tools such as:

SWOT Analysis

Identifies internal strengths and weaknesses, and external opportunities and threats.

PESTEL Analysis

Examines macro-environmental drivers:

- Political
- Economic
- Social
- Technological
- Environmental
- Legal

Game Theory Models

Used to understand competitive behavior, pricing strategies, collaboration, and conflict.

Value Chain Analysis

Identifies primary and support activities where value can be added or costs reduced.

These qualitative and analytical methods provide structured approaches for assessing competitive dynamics.

9.2.3 Quantitative Industry Modelling

Advanced quantitative techniques enhance empirical analysis and forecasting.

Econometric Modelling

Used for predicting market structure, industry demand, or strategic behaviour.

Survival Analysis

Helps estimate industry entry and exit patterns.

Demand Estimation Models

Logit and probit models support:

- Pricing decisions
- Consumer choice modelling
- Market segmentation

Data Envelopment Analysis (DEA)

Evaluates relative efficiency of firms using input-output relationships.

Such quantitative tools enable robust industry assessments and strategic decision-making.

9.3 Business Transformation Models

9.3.1 The Need for Transformation

Organizations face continuous change driven by:

- Digital disruption
- Globalization
- Regulatory evolution
- Shifting customer expectations

Transformation models help redesign organizational processes, structures, and culture to ensure long-term adaptability.

9.3.2 Popular Transformation Models

McKinsey 7-S Framework

Focuses on aligning seven internal elements:

- Strategy
- Structure
- Systems
- Skills

- Staff
- Style
- Shared Values

Kotter's 8-Step Model

Emphasizes:

- Creating urgency
- Building a guiding coalition
- Communicating the vision
- Empowering broad-based action
- Anchoring change in culture

ADKAR Model

Covers individual change across:

- Awareness
- Desire
- Knowledge
- Ability
- Reinforcement

Business Model Canvas

Visual tool for describing:

- Value proposition
- Customer segments
- Key partners and activities
- Revenue and cost structures

These frameworks guide both incremental and large-scale organizational transformation.

9.3.3 Digital Transformation Modelling

Digital transformation requires analytical frameworks that incorporate:

- AI/ML readiness assessments
- Cloud and data infrastructure maturity models
- Technology adoption curves
- System dynamics modelling of digital maturity
- Economic models to quantify ROI from digital investments

These tools help evaluate digital capabilities and guide prioritization of technology initiatives.

9.4 Scenario Planning for Long-Term Strategy

9.4.1 Purpose of Scenario Planning

Scenario planning is essential for navigating uncertainty caused by:

- Technological disruptions
- Market volatility
- Climate risks
- Policy and regulatory shifts

Its goals are to:

- Anticipate multiple future possibilities
- Develop flexible strategies
- Avoid strategic blind spots
- Prepare robust response plans

9.4.2 Scenario Modelling Process

Typical steps include:

1. Identify focal strategic issues
2. Analyze key driving forces (PESTEL)

3. Rank uncertainties by impact and unpredictability
4. Develop scenario frameworks (e.g., 2×2 matrices)
5. Quantify scenarios using forecasting tools
6. Evaluate strategic responses
7. Monitor leading indicators for early warning

Scenario modelling enhances strategic preparedness and resilience.

9.4.3 Quantitative Tools for Scenario Planning

- **Monte Carlo Simulation:** randomness-based modelling under uncertainty
- **Bayesian Networks:** probabilistic dependencies among variables
- **System Dynamics:** long-term simulation of feedback loops
- **Sensitivity Analysis:** evaluates strategic robustness under variations

These tools allow scenario planners to derive insights grounded in empirical modelling.

9.5 Integrating Strategic Models for Managerial Decision-Making

Strategic management modelling is most effective when integrated across different frameworks. Organizations often combine:

- **BSC** for performance measurement
- **Porter's tools** for industry positioning
- **Transformation models** for organizational alignment
- **Scenario planning** for future-proofing strategies

Modern decision-support systems incorporate these models into:

- Enterprise dashboards
- Predictive analytics platforms
- Simulation engines
- AI-driven strategic recommendation systems

Such integrated systems improve the quality of strategic decisions and enhance organizational agility.

Summary

This chapter provided a detailed overview of strategic modelling tools widely used in management and commerce. Through frameworks like the Balanced Scorecard, competitive analysis models, transformation models, and scenario planning techniques, organizations can strengthen strategic alignment, build resilience, and drive long-term value creation. When combined with modern analytics and decision-support systems, these models enable data-driven strategic decision-making in complex and dynamic business environments.

❐

Chapter 10

Digital Transformation & AI-Based Business Modelling

Keywords: Machine learning, decision automation, data mining, digital ecosystems, AI governance, decision intelligence.

Subject Classification:

- **JEL:** O33 (Technological Change), C45 (Neural Networks)
- **MSC:** 68T20 (Artificial Intelligence)
- **ACM CCS:** Artificial intelligence → Machine learning applications

Digital transformation has become a defining force reshaping global commerce, operational efficiency, and strategic decision-making. As organizations increasingly rely on data, automation, and intelligent systems, business modelling has evolved beyond traditional methods to incorporate artificial intelligence (AI), machine learning (ML), data mining, and advanced analytics. This chapter examines the role of AI-based models in commerce, customer analytics, decision automation, and pattern discovery, along with emerging ethical, legal, and governance challenges.

10.1 Machine Learning for Commerce

Machine learning provides organisations with highly accurate tools to model, predict, and optimize business processes. ML algorithms help uncover hidden patterns, automate repetitive functions, and forecast strategic outcomes.

10.1.1 Types of ML Used in Commerce

Supervised Learning

- **Regression:** sales forecasting, demand prediction, pricing models
- **Classification:** credit scoring, fraud detection, customer churn

Unsupervised Learning

- **Clustering:** market segmentation, customer grouping
- **Association Rules:** market basket analysis, cross-selling patterns

Reinforcement Learning

- Dynamic pricing
- Inventory optimization
- Real-time marketing recommendations

Semi-Supervised & Transfer Learning

Useful in contexts with limited labelled data (e.g., emerging markets, small enterprises).

10.1.2 ML Applications Across Business Functions

Finance

- Fraud detection
- Credit risk modelling

Marketing

- Lead scoring
- Targeted advertising
- Sentiment analysis

Operations & Supply Chain

- Demand forecasting
- Route optimization
- Predictive maintenance

Human Resources

- Automated CV screening
- Attrition prediction
- Skill matching

Retail & E-commerce

- Personalized product recommendations
- Inventory and assortment optimization

10.1.3 ML Workflow in Commerce

1. Data Acquisition
2. Data Cleaning and Feature Engineering
3. Algorithm Selection
4. Model Training & Validation
5. Deployment in Production Systems
6. Monitoring and Continuous Learning

ML systems today integrate seamlessly with ERP and CRM platforms, enabling real-time intelligent decision-making.

10.2 AI in Customer Prediction & Decision Automation

AI dramatically expands predictive capability by analyzing vast volumes of structured and unstructured customer data—purchase history, behavioural data, text feedback, social signals, and contextual information.

10.2.1 Customer Prediction Models

AI enables high-accuracy predictions such as:

- Customer churn and retention probability
- Purchase likelihood and next-best offer
- Customer lifetime value (CLV)
- Demand sensing and real-time demand detection
- Customer sentiment and satisfaction scoring

10.2.2 Recommendation Systems

Recommendation engines rely on:

- **Content-Based Filtering**
- **Collaborative Filtering**
- **Hybrid Models**

Business applications:

- E-commerce product recommendations
- Streaming/media content suggestions
- Personalized advertisements and promotions

These systems enhance customer experience and significantly raise conversion rates.

10.2.3 Decision Automation in Management

AI can autonomously execute routine and semi-structured decisions.

Examples:

- Automated credit approval using ML scoring models
- Dynamic pricing bots adjusting prices based on demand
- Automatic inventory replenishment
- AI-enabled chatbots and virtual agents

- Real-time managerial dashboards with predictive insights

Decision automation improves speed, accuracy, and consistency across large operational systems.

10.3 Data Mining & Pattern Discovery

Data mining extracts meaningful, actionable insights from large and complex datasets. It forms the analytical backbone of most digital transformation initiatives.

10.3.1 Key Data Mining Techniques

Classification & Regression

Predictive modelling for sales, risk, and performance.

Clustering

Grouping similar customers/products using k-means, hierarchical clustering, etc.

Association Rule Mining

Market basket analysis:

- "Customers who bought X also bought Y."

Text Mining & NLP

Extracting insights from:

- Emails
- Customer reviews
- Social media
- Support logs

Anomaly Detection

- Identifying unusual transactions, fraud, or system anomalies.

Sequence & Time-Series Mining

Studying event sequences, user behaviour flows, and temporal trends.

10.3.2 Business Applications

- **Retail:** demand patterns, promotion optimization, store layout planning
- **Banking:** suspicious transaction detection
- **Manufacturing:** defect and quality analysis
- **Marketing:** emerging trend detection
- **HR Analytics:** behavioural and performance pattern analysis

These applications support evidence-based decision-making, improving profitability and operational efficiency.

10.4 AI Ethics & Governance in Management Modelling

Widespread AI adoption introduces risks related to fairness, privacy, transparency, and accountability. Responsible governance is essential for sustainable AI integration.

10.4.1 Ethical Issues in AI

Bias & Discrimination

Biased data → unfair outcomes (e.g., hiring, credit scoring).

Privacy Violations

Unauthorized data usage or excessive surveillance.

Opacity ("Black-Box" Algorithms)

Difficulty interpreting deep learning models.

Job Displacement

Automation replacing routine work; need for workforce reskilling.

Algorithmic Manipulation

Unethical targeting, manipulation of consumer behaviour.

10.4.2 Governance Frameworks

Organizations must build formal governance structures:

AI Governance Committees

Cross-functional decision-making bodies.

Data Protection & Privacy Standards

Compliance with GDPR, PDPB (India), and global privacy laws.

Model Transparency & Explainability

Techniques include:

- SHAP
- LIME
- Interpretable ML

Risk Assessment & Audits

- Fairness audits
- Impact assessments
- Bias and discrimination testing

Cybersecurity Controls

Protecting AI models from tampering or adversarial attacks.

10.4.3 Ethical AI in Decision Support Systems

A responsible AI-based DSS must:

- Provide human-understandable explanations
- Maintain human-in-the-loop control for critical decisions

- Keep audit trails of decisions
- Monitor model performance for drift and degradation

Robust governance builds trust and ensures regulatory compliance.

10.5 Summary

Digital transformation and AI-based business modelling are reshaping how organizations create value, understand markets, and make decisions. Machine learning enhances prediction and operational efficiency, data mining uncovers hidden patterns, and AI-driven automation streamlines decision processes. However, as organizations rely increasingly on intelligent systems, ethical, transparent, and well-governed AI frameworks become essential. The most successful businesses will be those that combine innovation with accountability, ethics, and strategic oversight.

❒

Chapter 11

Risk, Uncertainty & Crisis Modelling

Keywords: Risk matrices, probability models, business continuity, credit risk, market risk, stress testing, scenario modelling

Subject Classification:

- **JEL:** G32 (Risk Management), D81 (Uncertainty)
- **MSC:** 91B30 (Risk theory)
- **ACM CCS:** Applied computing → Risk analysis

Risk and uncertainty are fundamental challenges in business analytics and decision-making. Organizations face a wide spectrum of potential disruptions—from financial volatility and operational failures to natural disasters and cyberattacks. To navigate such complexities, firms rely on structured risk modelling frameworks that quantify exposures, assess vulnerabilities, and guide the formulation of mitigation strategies. This chapter presents the major concepts and tools used in business risk assessment, business continuity planning, and crisis modelling.

11.1 Understanding Risk and Uncertainty in Business

Risk refers to measurable uncertainty, where the likelihood of outcomes can be estimated using probability distributions.

Uncertainty, in the Knightian sense, arises when probabilities are unknown or difficult to quantify.

Modern organizations face a variety of risk categories:

- **Strategic risks:** market shifts, competition, regulatory changes
- **Operational risks:** process failures, system breakdowns
- **Financial risks:** credit, market, liquidity risks
- **Compliance & regulatory risks:** legal penalties, reporting failures
- **Cybersecurity & data risks:** data breaches, ransomware
- **Environmental & disaster risks:** floods, pandemics, natural catastrophes

Risk modelling enhances organizational resilience by enabling anticipation, measurement, and mitigation of threats.

11.2 Risk Matrices and Probability Models

11.2.1 Risk Matrices

A **risk matrix** visually represents risks based on two dimensions:

- **Likelihood (Probability)**
- **Impact (Severity)**

Typical qualitative scales:

Likelihood: Rare → Unlikely → Possible → Likely → Almost Certain

Impact: Low → Medium → High → Critical

Interpretation:

- **High likelihood + high impact:** Critical zone (Red) – requires immediate action
- **Low likelihood + low impact:** Acceptable zone (Green)

Applications:

- Prioritizing mitigation efforts
- Supporting resource allocation
- Communicating risk levels to stakeholders

11.2.2 Probability Models for Risk Assessment

Expected Value (EV):

EV = P(event)×Impact

EV = P(\text{event})\times\text{Impact}

EV = P(event)×Impact

Probability Distributions:

- **Normal distribution:** market returns, natural variability
- **Poisson distribution:** rare events (e.g., machine failures)
- **Exponential distribution:** time to failure
- **Bernoulli/Binomial:** success–failure outcomes

Bayesian Modelling: Updates risk estimates as new information becomes available.

Fault Tree & Event Tree Analysis: Used in safety engineering and disaster studies to map pathways to failure or success.

These tools provide quantitative insights for preventive and corrective actions.

11.3 Business Continuity Modelling (BCM)

Business continuity modelling ensures that essential operations can continue during emergencies.

11.3.1 Key Components

- **Business Impact Analysis (BIA):** Identifies critical functions, downtime tolerances, dependencies.
- **Risk Assessment:** Identifies vulnerabilities in people, processes, and systems.
- **Continuity Strategies:** Redundancy, backups, supply chain alternatives, remote work options.
- **Disaster Recovery Planning (DRP):** Restoration of IT systems, data, and infrastructure.

11.3.2 BCM Modelling Techniques

- **Process Mapping:** Identifies process vulnerabilities.
- **Simulation Models:**
  - System dynamics for prolonged disruptions
  - Monte Carlo simulation for probabilistic failures
  - Agent-based models for crisis behaviour
- **Network Analysis:** Examines supply chain robustness.
- **Reliability Models:** MTBF, MTTR, uptime modelling.

BCM helps prevent operational paralysis and supports rapid recovery.

11.4 Credit Risk and Market Risk Models

11.4.1 Credit Risk Modelling

Credit risk reflects the likelihood of borrower default.

Common tools:

- **Credit Scoring Models:** Logistic regression, decision trees, ML models
- **Altman Z-score:** Corporate bankruptcy prediction

- **Credit Metrics:** Portfolio credit risk estimation
- **PD, LGD, EAD models:** Core regulatory parameters
- **Transition Matrices:** Track rating migrations over time

11.4.2 Market Risk Modelling

Market risk arises from fluctuations in financial variables such as interest rates, stock prices, and exchange rates.

Core models:

- **Value at Risk (VaR):**
  - Historical simulation
  - Variance–covariance
  - Monte Carlo simulation
- **Expected Shortfall (ES):** Tail-risk measure more conservative than VaR.
- **GARCH Models:** Volatility modelling in turbulent markets.
- **Black–Scholes and derivatives pricing models:** Quantify risks in options and futures positions.

These models support financial institutions in regulatory compliance and risk mitigation.

11.5 Stress Testing and Scenario Modelling

11.5.1 Stress Testing Approaches

Stress testing evaluates resilience under *extreme but plausible* conditions.

Types:

- **Sensitivity Analysis:** Adjust one variable (e.g., interest rates) to observe effects.

- **Reverse Stress Testing:** Identify conditions that could cause failure.
- **Regulatory Stress Testing:** As required under Basel or central bank guidelines.

Examples of stress scenarios:

- Sudden market crashes
- Supply chain disruptions
- Pandemic-like shocks
- Geopolitical crises
- Currency volatility

11.5.2 Scenario Modelling

Scenario modelling involves constructing structured narratives and quantifying their impacts.

Steps:

1. Identify key risk drivers
2. Determine uncertainties
3. Develop scenario narratives (best/base/worst cases)
4. Quantify impacts using econometric, forecasting, or simulation models
5. Formulate response strategies
6. Monitor early-warning indicators

11.5.3 Quantitative Tools for Scenarios

- Monte Carlo simulation
- System dynamics
- Bayesian networks
- Agent-based models

- Macroeconomic VAR models
- Scenario modelling strengthens long-term resilience and crisis preparedness.

11.6 Summary

Risk, uncertainty, and crisis modelling form a core component of strategic and operational resilience. Using risk matrices and probability-based tools, organizations can quantify threats and prioritize mitigation actions. Business continuity modelling ensures operational survival during disruptions, while credit and market risk models support financial stability and regulatory compliance. Stress testing and scenario modelling help organizations anticipate extreme events and design adaptive strategies. Together, these methods create a robust framework for managing uncertainty in modern commercial environments.

❐

Chapter 12

Sustainability, ESG & Social Impact Modelling

Keywords: Environmental modelling, ESG metrics, circular economy, SROI, sustainable operations, carbon modelling

Subject Classification:

- **JEL:** Q01 (Sustainability), M14 (Corporate Social Responsibility)
- **MSC:** 62P12 (Environmental statistics)
- **ACM CCS:** Applied computing → Environmental sciences

Sustainability has become a strategic imperative for modern organizations. Driven by increasing regulatory requirements, stakeholder expectations, and urgent global challenges—including climate change, biodiversity loss, and social inequality—businesses are investing in quantitative and qualitative models to evaluate their environmental, social, and governance (ESG) performance. Sustainability modelling offers a systematic approach for measuring impacts, reducing risks, and ensuring long-term value creation. This chapter discusses key frameworks and analytical tools, including environmental impact models, ESG performance metrics, circular economy modelling, and social return on investment (SROI).

12.1 Environmental Impact Models

Environmental impact models quantify the ecological consequences of products, processes, supply chains, and organizational operations. These models guide firms in reducing emissions, conserving resources, and improving environmental stewardship.

12.1.1 Life Cycle Assessment (LCA)

Life Cycle Assessment evaluates the environmental footprint of a product or service across its complete life cycle:

- Raw material extraction
- Manufacturing and processing
- Transportation and distribution
- Use and maintenance
- End-of-life disposal, recycling, or recovery

Common LCA indicators:

- Carbon footprint (CO_{2e})
- Water footprint
- Total energy consumption
- Waste generation
- Ecotoxicity and pollution impact

LCA supports eco-design, green innovation, and sustainable supply chain management.

12.1.2 Carbon Accounting & Emission Modelling

Organizations increasingly measure and manage their greenhouse gas (GHG) emissions across:

- **Scope 1:** Direct emissions from controlled sources
- **Scope 2:** Indirect emissions from purchased electricity
- **Scope 3:** Upstream and downstream value-chain emissions

Modelling techniques include:

- Emission factor–based calculations
- Time-series forecasting of carbon emissions
- Monte Carlo analysis for uncertainty quantification
- Marginal Abatement Cost Curves (MACC) for evaluating reduction strategies

Carbon accounting is central to climate strategies, regulatory compliance, and net-zero commitments.

12.1.3 Environmental Risk Modelling

Environmental risks include climate-related hazards, regulatory shifts, resource scarcity, and biodiversity decline.

Modelling tools:

- **Climate scenario models** (e.g., IPCC pathways for 1.5°C/2°C futures)
- **GIS-based spatial models** for flood, drought, and heatwave risk
- **Ecological footprint calculators** for resource consumption analysis

These models support proactive adaptation and resilience planning.

12.2 ESG Performance Metrics

Environmental, Social, and Governance (ESG) metrics are widely used by investors, regulators, and rating agencies to evaluate sustainability performance.

12.2.1 ESG Frameworks and Standards

Major global frameworks include:

- Global Reporting Initiative (GRI)
- Sustainability Accounting Standards Board (SASB)

- Task Force on Climate-Related Financial Disclosures (TCFD)
- Integrated Reporting (<IR>) Framework
- UN Sustainable Development Goals (SDGs)

These standards harmonize reporting, enhance transparency, and guide responsible investment.

12.2.2 Environmental Metrics

- GHG emissions (Scopes 1–3)
- Water use efficiency
- Renewable energy share
- Waste recycling and diversion rates
- Pollution and environmental compliance metrics

12.2.3 Social Metrics

- Employee safety, health, and well-being
- Diversity, equity, and inclusion (DEI) indicators
- Community engagement and investment
- Human rights performance
- Customer satisfaction and product quality

12.2.4 Governance Metrics

- Board independence and diversity
- Anti-corruption and ethical governance
- Transparency and disclosure quality
- Data privacy and cybersecurity governance
- Executive compensation alignment

12.2.5 ESG Scoring & Rating Models

Organizations and investors use:

- Weighted ESG indices

- Industry-benchmark scoring models
- Machine learning algorithms for disclosure analysis
- Multi-criteria decision analysis (MCDA)

ESG scoring influences capital allocation, risk assessment, and long-term strategic planning.

12.3 Circular Economy Modelling

The circular economy aims to replace the linear take–make–dispose model with a system emphasizing resource circularity, efficiency, and regeneration.

12.3.1 Principles of the Circular Economy

- Waste minimization
- Resource efficiency
- Product life extension
- Recycling, recovery, and remanufacturing
- Closed-loop supply chains
- Regenerative and restorative design

12.3.2 Circular Economy Models

- **Material Flow Analysis (MFA):** Tracks material inputs, outputs, and leakages.
- **Input–Output Models:** Examine environmental impacts across industries.
- **Closed-Loop Supply Chain Models:** Optimize reverse logistics, remanufacturing, and recycling.
- **Product-as-a-Service (PaaS) Models:** Use analytics to manage product lifespan and maintenance cycles.
- **Waste-to-Value Models:** Convert waste streams into revenue-generating resources.

12.3.3 Tools and Techniques

- System dynamics simulation
- LCA integrated with circular indicators
- Optimization models (linear/mixed-integer programming)
- Digital twins for resource-flow monitoring

Circular economy modelling supports cost reduction, innovation, and enhanced sustainability performance.

12.4 Social Return on Investment (SROI)

Social Return on Investment (SROI) quantifies the social, economic, and environmental value created by programs or initiatives.

12.4.1 Concept and Purpose

SROI compares:

SROI Ratio=Total Social Benefits Total Resources Invested\text{SROI Ratio} = \frac{\text{Total Social Benefits}}{\text{Total Resources Invested}}SROI Ratio = Total Resources Invested Total Social Benefits

It enables organizations to assess:

- Social value creation
- Community impact
- Effectiveness of CSR programs
- Public policy outcomes
- Justification for funding and investment

12.4.2 Types of SROI

- **Evaluative SROI:** Based on outcomes already achieved
- **Forecast SROI:** Predicts future impact before implementation

12.4.3 Steps in SROI Modelling

1. Identify stakeholders
2. Map inputs, outputs, and outcomes
3. Assign monetary values to outcomes
4. Adjust for deadweight, displacement, attribution, and drop-off
5. Calculate the SROI ratio
6. Interpret results and prepare reports

12.4.4 Applications

- Education and skill-development programs
- Healthcare and well-being initiatives
- Microfinance and poverty alleviation
- Nonprofit and social enterprise evaluation
- Government public policy assessments
- SROI aligns social investments with measurable, meaningful impact.

12.5 Summary

Sustainability and ESG modelling are essential components of responsible and future-oriented management. Environmental impact models such as LCA and carbon accounting help quantify ecological footprints. ESG metrics provide structured frameworks to assess corporate sustainability performance across environmental, social, and governance dimensions. Circular economy models enable resource-efficient and regenerative systems, promoting innovation and long-term resilience. SROI offers a powerful tool to measure, evaluate, and monetize social value creation.

❐

Chapter 13
Integrated Enterprise Modelling & Business Architecture**

Keywords: Enterprise architecture, process modelling, BPMN, value stream mapping, ERP-based modelling, digital twins

Subject Classification:

- **JEL:** M15 (IT Management), O32 (Technology Systems)
- **MSC:** 68U35 (Information Systems)
- **ACM CCS:** Applied computing → Enterprise modelling

13.0 Introduction

Modern organizations operate in highly interconnected and data-intensive environments. To remain competitive, business processes, technology systems, data structures, and organizational capabilities must be designed holistically. **Integrated enterprise modelling** provides the foundation for this alignment, while **business architecture** offers a high-level blueprint for capabilities, value streams, workflows, and information systems.

This chapter explores key enterprise modelling frameworks, process modelling techniques such as BPMN and Value Stream Mapping, ERP-based modelling methodologies, and the rapidly expanding role of **digital twins** in commerce.

13.1 Enterprise Modelling Frameworks

Enterprise modelling frameworks help structure organizational information, strategy, and workflows. They provide a systematic view of operations and guide digital transformation.

13.1.1 The Zachman Framework

A taxonomy-based framework structured across:

- **Perspectives:** Planner, Owner, Designer, Builder, User, Enterprise
- **Dimensions:** Data, Function, Network, People, Time, Motivation

It provides a matrix for documenting enterprise artefacts and maintaining architectural consistency.

13.1.2 TOGAF (The Open Group Architecture Framework)

TOGAF is one of the most widely adopted architecture frameworks. Its core is the **Architecture Development Method (ADM)**, which guides iterative architecture creation.

Key Components:

- Architecture Development Method (ADM)
- Enterprise Continuum
- Architecture Capability Framework

It integrates business, application, data, and technology architectures.

13.1.3 FEAF (Federal Enterprise Architecture Framework)

Used primarily in government and public-sector institutions.

It aligns:

- Business architecture
- Data standards

- Applications and shared services
- Performance metrics

FEAF emphasizes standardization, interoperability, and governance.

13.1.4 Integrated Enterprise Modelling (IEM) Methodology

Focuses on interlinking:

- Organizational goals
- Business processes
- Resource modelling
- Information flow modelling

IEM creates a coherent view across functional, informational, and technical layers.

13.1.5 Capability-Based Modelling

A capability represents what an organization can do, independent of processes or systems.

Steps:

1. Identify strategic capabilities
2. Assess capability maturity
3. Map capabilities to processes, people, and IT systems
4. Prioritize improvements

Capability modelling supports strategic planning and investment decision-making.

13.2 Process Modelling (BPMN and Value Stream Mapping)

Process modelling represents business operations to identify inefficiencies, improve performance, and enable automation.

13.2.1 Business Process Model and Notation (BPMN)

BPMN provides a globally standardized notation for modelling workflows.

Core Elements:

- **Events:** start, intermediate, end
- **Activities:** tasks, subprocesses
- **Gateways:** AND, OR, XOR
- **Flows:** sequence and message flows
- **Pools/Lanes:** represent roles, actors, or departments

Applications:

- Workflow automation
- Process redesign
- ERP/CRM integration
- Business Process Management Systems (BPMS)

13.2.2 Value Stream Mapping (VSM)

A Lean tool that maps the flow of value through a system.

Key Components:

- Value-adding and non-value-adding steps
- Material flow
- Information flow
- Lead time and cycle time
- Inventory and waiting periods

VSM is ideal for supply chain optimization, lean operations, and continuous improvement.

13.2.3 BPMN vs. VSM

Feature	BPMN	VSM
Focus	Workflow logic	Value flow & waste
Method	Standardized notation	Lean philosophy
Use Cases	Automation, integration	Process improvement
Detail	High technical detail	Operational metrics

Both tools complement each other in enterprise transformation.

13.3 ERP-Based Business Modelling

Enterprise Resource Planning (ERP) systems integrate key business functions into a unified platform. ERP modelling ensures that organizational processes align effectively with ERP capabilities.

13.3.1 ERP Architecture

Common modules include:

- Finance & Accounting
- Supply Chain & Logistics
- Procurement
- Human Resources
- Manufacturing
- Sales & CRM

13.3.2 ERP Process Modelling

Key steps:

1. **As-Is Process Mapping**

   Document existing workflows.

2. **To-Be Process Design**

   Define improved workflows based on ERP best practices.

3. **Gap Analysis**

   Compare current processes with ERP functionalities.

4. **Configuration & Customization Modelling**

   Configure ERP modules to organizational needs.

13.3.3 Benefits of ERP-Based Modelling

- Standardized processes
- Real-time data flow
- Improved accuracy & transparency
- Enhanced planning & control
- Scalability and compliance

13.3.4 ERP Simulation Models

Used for:

- Inventory management
- Production planning
- Financial forecasting
- Capacity and demand analysis

Simulations help test process performance before implementation.

13.4 Digital Twins for Commerce

Digital twins are virtual replicas of physical or logical systems, connected through real-time data streams.

13.4.1 Components of a Digital Twin

1. Physical Entity (store, warehouse, supply chain)
2. Digital Model
3. Data Integration Layer (ERP, IoT sensors, CRM)
4. Analytics & Simulation Engine

13.4.2 Types of Digital Twins

- **Product Twins** – product performance behaviour
- **Process Twins** – manufacturing/service workflows
- **Operational Twins** – logistics/warehouse operations
- **Enterprise Twins** – holistic business ecosystem

13.4.3 Applications in Commerce

Retail and Customer Behaviour

- Footfall prediction
- Virtual store layout experiments
- Demand simulation

Supply Chain & Logistics

- Route optimization
- Inventory balancing
- Predictive maintenance

Finance & Risk

- Cash-flow forecasting
- Fraud detection
- Scenario modelling

Omnichannel Experience

- Cross-channel customer journey mapping
- Personalization using behavioural analytics

13.4.4 Benefits of Digital Twins

- Real-time decision-making
- Predictive accuracy
- Faster scenario testing

- Operational agility
- Innovation acceleration

13.5 Summary

Integrated enterprise modelling and business architecture enable organizations to achieve strategic alignment, operational efficiency, and digital readiness. Frameworks such as Zachman, TOGAF, and FEAF provide architectural clarity. BPMN and VSM support the visual analysis and improvement of workflows. ERP-based modelling aligns systems and processes for unified operations. Digital twins bring unprecedented predictive and real-time analytical capabilities.

Together, these tools empower modern enterprises to innovate, optimize, and compete effectively in dynamic markets.

❐

Chapter 14
Applications of Modelling in International Commerce

Keywords: Trade flow modelling, exchange rate modelling, global supply networks, cross-border e-commerce, currency risk, logistics modelling

Subject Classification:

- **JEL:** F10 (International Trade), F31 (Exchange Rates)
- **MSC:** 91B26 (Market models), 91B74 (International trade models)
- **ACM CCS:** Applied computing → International business

14.0 Introduction

International commerce is shaped by complex interactions among global supply chains, exchange rate movements, cross-border consumer behaviour, and international regulations. For firms operating across borders, **modelling and analytics** are essential for understanding trade flows, managing risk, forecasting demand, and optimising logistics.

This chapter presents key modelling approaches used in international trade analysis, currency risk management, global supply network optimisation, and cross-border e-commerce analytics.

14.1 Trade Flow Modelling

Trade flow models help analysts and policymakers understand how goods, services, and capital move between nations.

14.1.1 The Gravity Model of International Trade

The gravity model explains bilateral trade based on the economic size and distance between trading countries. The basic form is:

Tradeij=GGDPi·GDPjDistanceijβ

Trade_{ij} = G \frac{GDP_i \cdot GDP_j} {Distance_{ij}^{\beta}}

Tradeij = GDistanceijβGDPi·GDPj

Where:

- G = gravitational constant
- GDPi,GDPj = economic mass of the countries
- Distance ij Distance_{ij}Distanceij = geographical/ economic distance
- β\betaβ = distance elasticity

Applications:

- Export market selection
- Evaluating trade agreements
- Tariff/NTM (non-tariff measure) analysis
- Identifying potential trade partners
- Predicting bilateral trade potential

14.1.2 Input–Output and Global Value Chain Models

These models capture cross-country production fragmentation and intermediate goods trade.

Uses:

- Estimating value-added contributions across countries
- Understanding offshoring and outsourcing effects
- Analysing vulnerability in global supply chains

14.1.3 Trade Forecasting Models

Forecasting tools include ARIMA, regression models, structural econometric models, and machine learning.

Important predictors:

- Global GDP growth
- Commodity prices
- Exchange rate trends
- Freight and shipping index behaviour

Trade forecasting supports strategic planning for exporters and importers.

14.2 Currency Risk & Exchange Rate Modelling

Exchange rate fluctuations significantly impact pricing, profits, and global competitiveness.

14.2.1 Econometric Models

Common analytical tools:

- **ARIMA/ARIMAX** – short-term price forecasting
- **GARCH** – modelling volatility clustering
- **VAR** – macroeconomic interdependence analysis

Applications:

- Hedging using forward contracts, options, and swaps
- Export and import price setting
- Cash flow and treasury risk planning

14.2.2 Purchasing Power Parity (PPP) & Interest Rate Parity (IRP)

Used for determining long-term equilibrium exchange rates.

Applications:

- Detecting currency misalignment
- Competitiveness benchmarking
- Policy analysis for macroeconomic stability

14.2.3 Machine Learning Models for FX Prediction

Advanced ML techniques capture nonlinear patterns in exchange rates.

Useful models:

- Random Forests
- LSTM neural networks
- Gradient Boosting models

Key inputs:

- Market sentiment indicators
- News and social media analytics
- Commodity and macroeconomic variables

14.3 Global Supply Network Modelling

Global supply networks require careful optimisation across suppliers, plants, warehouses, and transport channels.

14.3.1 Supply Network Optimization Models

Key methodologies:

- **Mixed-Integer Linear Programming (MILP)**
- **Cost-to-serve and landed cost models**
- **Risk-adjusted supply chain modelling**

Uses:

- Choosing supplier and factory locations
- Evaluating nearshoring/offshoring strategies
- Minimising tariffs, duties, and logistics costs

14.3.2 Multi-Echelon Inventory Modelling

Multinational supply chains span multiple layers:

- Central hubs
- Regional DCs
- Local retail/fulfilment nodes

Models determine:

- Safety stock allocation
- Lead time variability buffers
- Cross-border replenishment strategies

14.3.3 Global Logistics Routing Models

Includes:

- International Vehicle Routing Problem (VRP)
- Maritime and air cargo optimisation
- Intermodal models integrating sea–rail–road–air

Applications:

- Lowering transit time and carbon footprint
- Avoiding port congestion
- Ensuring global delivery service levels

14.4 Cross-Border E-Commerce Analytics

Cross-border e-commerce has democratized global trade, enabling SMEs to access international consumers at low cost.

14.4.1 Modelling Consumer Behaviour Across Countries

Factors:

- Cultural preferences
- Purchasing power differentials
- Payment method preferences
- Festival and season-linked behaviour

Model types:

- Segmentation and clustering
- Country-level demand forecasting
- Recommendation systems

14.4.2 Pricing & Competition Modelling

Tools:

- Dynamic pricing algorithms
- FX-adjusted international pricing
- Competitor price tracking models

14.4.3 Cross-Border Fraud & Risk Modelling

Machine learning identifies:

- Suspicious transaction patterns
- Geolocation anomalies
- High-risk purchase behaviour
- Chargeback probabilities

14.4.4 Cross-Border Logistics & Delivery Optimisation

Models assist with:

- Last-mile delivery across country borders
- Optimizing customs clearance time
- Predicting delivery delays
- Handling international returns

14.5 Case Applications in International Commerce

Case 1: Global Retail Expansion

A global retailer uses:

- Gravity models for market selection

- Consumer segmentation models for localisation
- Network optimisation for regional warehouse placement

Case 2: Pharmaceutical Supply Chain Resilience

After pandemic disruptions, a multinational drug manufacturer applies:

- Simulation modelling
- MILP network optimisation
- Cold-chain temperature risk modelling
- To redesign a robust global distribution network.

Case 3: Cross-Border Digital Marketplace

An online marketplace applies:

- Exchange rate–adjusted dynamic pricing
- ML-based fraud detection
- Regional recommendation engines

To support millions of international transactions daily.

14.6 Summary

Modelling in international commerce empowers firms to navigate global uncertainty with scientific precision.

Key contributions include:

- Improved understanding of global trade patterns
- Better management of exchange rate volatility
- Optimised global supply chains
- Data-driven strategies for cross-border e-commerce

In an increasingly interconnected world, these modelling tools enhance global competitiveness, reduce operational risk, and support strategic decision-making.

❒

Chapter 15
Future Directions in Management & Commerce Modelling

Keywords: Predictive enterprise, autonomous decision systems, behavioural economics, nudging, post-digital commerce, AI-driven strategies

Subject Classification:

- **JEL:** O30 (Innovation), D90 (Behavioural Decision Models)
- **MSC:** 68T40 (Artificial intelligence applications), 91Fxx (Future systems)
- **ACM CCS:** Computing methodologies → Intelligent systems

15.0 Introduction

Management and commerce are entering an era shaped by **hyper-connectivity**, **algorithmic decision-making**, and **human–AI collaboration**. Classical modelling—based on econometrics, optimisation, and simulation—is rapidly evolving into systems powered by **machine learning**, **real-time data**, **behavioural science**, and **autonomous agents**.

Organisations are transitioning from *descriptive* to *predictive*, and ultimately to *self-optimising*, **autonomous** decision environments.

This chapter outlines forward-looking modelling paradigms that will define the next generation of enterprise systems and commerce ecosystems.

15.1 Predictive Enterprises

A predictive enterprise uses real-time analytics, continuous learning models, and automation to anticipate outcomes and optimise decisions before disruptions occur.

15.1.1 Characteristics of Predictive Enterprises

- **Real-time data ecosystems:** IoT sensors, ERP and CRM streams, digital footprints
- **Proactive decision intelligence:** Predictive dashboards, anomaly detection, forecasting engines
- **Continuous learning:** ML models retrained with new data
- **Predictive operations:** Asset failure forecasting, workforce attrition prediction
- **Scenario simulation:** Enterprise digital twins for planning under uncertainty

15.1.2 Predictive Modelling Tools

- ML-based time-series forecasting (Prophet, LSTM, hybrid models)
- Predictive maintenance and asset failure models
- Customer churn prediction and lifetime value modelling
- Market trend prediction using news analytics and global signals
- Enterprise-level digital twins for system-wide forecasting

15.1.3 Strategic Benefits

- Reduced operational risk
- Stronger resilience to market disruptions
- Improved customer satisfaction and retention
- Higher resource utilisation
- Faster and more reliable decision cycles

15.2 Autonomous Decision Systems

Autonomous decision systems (ADS) represent the next stage: systems that **not only predict but act**—with limited human intervention.

15.2.1 Core Technologies

- **Reinforcement Learning (RL):** Agents learn optimal actions through rewards
- **Autonomous software agents:** For dynamic pricing, routing, procurement
- **Self-optimising supply chains:** Automated inventory, replenishment, and logistics
- **Cognitive automation:** NLP-based systems analysing contracts, emails, compliance data
- **Control systems:** Feedback loops enabling continuous adjustment

15.2.2 Applications in Management

- **Autonomous inventory planning:** AI triggers reorders using demand signals
- **Dynamic pricing engines:** Real-time price changes based on elasticity
- **Self-operating marketing campaigns:** AI optimises targeting, content, and bidding

- **AI-managed financial portfolios:** Automated rebalancing based on volatility and risk
- **Smart contract–driven procurement:** Automated vendor payments and approvals

15.2.3 Governance & Ethical Challenges

- Transparency and explainability of AI decisions
- Regulatory compliance for automated actions
- Human–AI collaboration protocols
- Safe boundaries for autonomous behaviours
- Bias, fairness, and ethical risk in automated processes

15.3 Behavioural Economics & Nudging Models

Behavioural economics integrates psychology into modelling, explaining real-world choices better than classical rational models.

15.3.1 Behavioural Assumptions

Decision-makers exhibit:

- Limited rationality
- Cognitive biases (anchoring, loss aversion, framing effects)
- Social influence and emotional drivers
- Rule-of-thumb (heuristic) behaviour
- Non-linear preference patterns

15.3.2 Nudging Models in Management

Nudges subtly influence choices without restricting freedom.

Applications:

- **Employee nudges:** Goal framing, productivity reminders, progress dashboards

- **Customer nudges:** Scarcity cues, social proof, personalised recommendations
- **Financial nudges:** Auto-enrolment, savings prompts, default settings
- **Health & wellness nudges:** Step goals, nutrition alerts, habit reinforcement

15.3.3 Behavioural Modelling Techniques

- Prospect theory decision functions
- Behavioural simulation models
- A/B testing frameworks
- Behavioural clustering for segmentation
- Predictive behavioural analytics

Behavioural modelling is essential for human-centric systems in marketing, HR, finance, and public policy.

15.4 Modelling for Post-Digital Commerce Ecosystems

In the **post-digital era**, digital technologies are ubiquitous—embedded into every interaction. Models must capture decentralisation, platform effects, and immersive environments.

15.4.1 Characteristics of Post-Digital Commerce

- Hyper-personalised experiences
- Continuous human–AI collaboration
- Platform and ecosystem dominance
- Ultra-fast digital experimentation
- Blockchain and Web3 integration
- Ubiquitous data and pervasive computing

15.4.2 Next-Generation Modelling Approaches

a. **Platform Ecosystem Modelling**
   - Multi-sided market models
   - Network effect simulations
   - Viral growth and diffusion modelling
   - Platform governance optimisation

b. **Blockchain & Decentralised Commerce Models**
   - Smart contract lifecycle modelling
   - Token economy simulations
   - Trust, identity, and verification models
   - Blockchain-enabled supply chain tracking

c. **Metaverse & Immersive Commerce**
   - Avatar-based consumer behaviour modelling
   - Immersive environment analytics
   - 3D product interaction metrics
   - Virtual economy modelling

d. **AI-Augmented Supply Chain Models**
   - Real-time, self-learning digital twins
   - Intelligent routing and logistics
   - Dynamic and predictive network optimisation

15.4.3 Sustainability & Circular Economy Integration

- Future commerce ecosystems require:
- Carbon-aware supply chains
- ESG dashboards embedded into decision systems
- Circular flow modelling and closed-loop networks
- Green logistics and carbon-minimisation algorithms

15.5 Summary and Future Outlook

The future of management and commerce modelling will be shaped by:

- A transition from **predictive** to **autonomous** decision systems
- Deeper integration of **behavioural insights**, making models more human-centric
- Expansion of **digital twins**, immersive analytics, and real-time optimization
- A shift toward **platform, blockchain, and Web3-based commerce ecosystems**
- Embedding sustainability and ethical governance into modelling frameworks

Future research scopes (concise, actionable)

Below are focused, publishable research directions you can take from the manuscript's themes. Each item includes a short research question, suggested methods, and why it matters — with recent literature pointers.

1. Hybrid MCDM frameworks tuned for socio-mathematical problems

Research question: How can hybrid Fuzzy-AHP + Fuzzy-TOPSIS (or similar ensembles) be adapted to capture evolving social preferences and non-stationary weights in organizations?

Methods: dynamic/hierarchical FAHP for weight elicitation; Fuzzy-TOPSIS for ranking; bootstrap or Bayesian updating of fuzzy weights; real-world case studies (HR selection, supplier choice).

Why it matters: hybrid MCDM remains a leading practical approach for subjective multi-criteria decisions; recent work shows hybrid FAHP–TOPSIS continues to be effective and widely adopted. MDPI+1

2. Fuzzy forecasting that integrates hesitancy and neural methods

Research question: Can hesitant fuzzy time-series models combined with neural architectures (LSTM/Transformer) improve forecasting under ambiguous demand and human-behavior signals?

Methods: hesitant fuzzy time series (HFTS), feature engineering using fuzzy granulation, hybrid HFTS + LSTM or fuzzy-neuro ensembles, cross-validation on real demand / enrollment datasets.

Why it matters: fuzzy time-series methods handle non-linearity and ambiguity better than crisp methods; integrating them with deep learning can combine interpretability with predictive power. ResearchGate+1

3. Fuzzy Cognitive Maps (FCMs) for organizational policy simulation and scenario planning

Research question: How can FCMs (and their learning extensions) model causal, fuzzy relationships among informal networks, morale, and performance to test policy interventions?

Methods: build FCMs from expert elicitation and data; use learning algorithms to tune weights; run scenario analyses and sensitivity studies; compare with system dynamics/agent-based models.

Why it matters: FCMs are well-suited to capture causal beliefs and fuzzy influence among socio-organizational variables; extensions and learning methods are actively developing. ACM Digital Library+1

4. Higher-order/type-3 and interval-valued fuzzy systems for richer uncertainty modelling

Research question: Do Type-3 or interval-valued fuzzy systems produce materially better decision support in highly ambiguous managerial contexts (e.g., public policy, crisis management) than Type-1/Type-2 systems?

Methods: implement Type-1, Type-2, and Type-3 controllers/classifiers on identical problem sets (e.g., workforce allocation in crisis), compare robustness and interpretability.

Why it matters: Type-3 and higher-order fuzzy systems are emerging as a way to encode additional layers of uncertainty and produce more robust control/decisions. IEEE Journal of Autonomous Systems

5. Socio-mathematical graph models: intuitionistic & fuzzy influence graphs for social network analysis

Research question: How can intuitionistic or interval fuzzy graphs capture influence plus non-influence (membership and non-membership) in organizational networks to predict information diffusion or resistance?

Methods: develop Intuitionistic Fuzzy Influence Graphs (IFIGs), compute centralities and coverings, validate on academic/enterprise social network data (email, collaboration).

Why it matters: such models embed richer uncertainty about ties and influence, improving predictions of diffusion and response to interventions. MDPI+1

6. Explainability & interpretability of fuzzy-augmented ML in managerial settings

Research question: How can fuzzy logic be combined with ML to produce decision outputs that managers trust and can audit (e.g., transparent fuzzy rules, counterfactual explanations)?

Methods: fuzzy rule extraction from models, local interpretable fuzzy explanations, human-in-the-loop evaluation studies measuring trust and usability.

Why it matters: managers require explainable outputs; recent surveys highlight growing interest in fuzzy methods for interpretability in ML. ScienceDirect

7. Ethical frameworks and fairness under fuzziness

Research question: How to operationalize "fairness" when eligibility, merit, or risk are fuzzy (e.g., partially eligible, borderline cases)?

Methods: define fuzzy fairness metrics (membership-based parity), test policy simulations (resource allocation), include stakeholder preferences via fuzzy MCDM.

Why it matters: ethical decisions in organizations are rarely binary; fuzzy fairness offers nuanced policy levers and audit trails. (Relevant intersection of fuzzy MCDM and socio-ethical policy design.)

8. Human-centered measurement: converting linguistic judgments into validated fuzzy metrics

Research question: What elicitation protocols and aggregation methods produce reliable, low-bias fuzzy metrics for constructs like trust, motivation, and leadership?

Methods: comparative experiments on linguistic scales vs. numeric scales; calibrate membership functions using anchored vignettes; validate against behavioral outcomes.

Why it matters: converging subjective responses into operational measures is critical for credible fuzzy performance systems.

Pragmatic next steps & datasets/methods suggestions

- **Datasets:** organizational surveys (employee engagement, eNPS), enterprise communication logs (anonymized email metadata), retail demand/ enrollment time series, policy decision datasets.
- **Method stacks:** FAHP/FTOPSIS, Hesitant FTS + LSTM, FCM + learning (e.g., differential Hebbian/ gradient methods), Type-2/Type-3 fuzzy controllers, intuitionistic fuzzy graphs.
- **Evaluation:** combine predictive metrics (RMSE, MAE) with decision-quality metrics (regret, stakeholder satisfaction), and user studies for explainability/trust.

Glossary (practical definitions + short pointer to a recent source where useful)

1. **Fuzzy set/membership function** — A set where elements have degrees of membership $\mu(x) \in [0,1]$, representing partial belonging rather than crisp inclusion. (Foundational concept used across methods.)

   (No single new ref — standard in fuzzy literature.)

2. **Type-1/Type-2/Type-3 fuzzy systems** —
   - *Type-1:* membership functions are crisp values in [0,1].
   - *Type-2:* membership functions themselves carry uncertainty (a fuzzy set of membership values).
   - *Type-3:* a higher-order generalization that can model yet another layer of uncertainty/imperfection; survey of Type-3 systems and trends highlights recent interest. IEEE Journal of Autonomous Systems.

3. **Intuitionistic fuzzy set** — Each element has a membership and non-membership degree (and hesitation margin), useful to model both support and opposition simultaneously. (Applied in fuzzy social graphs; see recent modeling of academic social networks.) MDPI
4. **Hesitant fuzzy set/hesitant fuzzy time series (HFTS)** — Used when experts hesitate among several membership degrees; HFTS extends fuzzy time series to capture such hesitancy and has been applied to forecasting ambiguous series. ScienceDirect+1
5. **Fuzzy AHP (FAHP)** — Analytic Hierarchy Process augmented with fuzzy numbers to allow imprecise pairwise comparisons; commonly used to derive weights when judgments are subjective. Hybrid FAHP + TOPSIS is widely used for MCDM. MDPI+1
6. **Fuzzy TOPSIS (FTOPSIS)** — Technique for order preference by similarity to ideal solution, adapted to fuzzy values; often paired with FAHP for weights. Wiley Online Library
7. **Fuzzy Cognitive Map (FCM)** — A graph-based causal model where concepts (nodes) influence each other with fuzzy weights; useful for "what if" policy simulation and modeling soft causal beliefs. Recent systematic reviews document many extensions and learning methods. ACM Digital Library+1
8. **Granulation/interval partitioning** — Dividing continuous variable ranges into fuzzy intervals (granules) for constructing fuzzy time series or linguistic variables; a key preprocessing step in many fuzzy forecasting pipelines. MDPI+1

9. **Socio-mathematical model** — Mathematical models (graphs, fuzzy graphs, influence graphs) that explicitly represent social relations, norms, and influence with formal uncertainty treatment (e.g., fuzzy or intuitionistic fuzzy ties). MDPI+1
10. **Explainable fuzzy-ML** — Hybrid approaches that extract human-readable fuzzy rules from ML or incorporate fuzzy logic to improve interpretability and trust. Recent surveys highlight increasing attention to fuzzy explainability in ML. ScienceDirect

Selected recent references (short list — good starting points)

1. Tran, N.T., *An Integrated Approach of Fuzzy AHP-TOPSIS for Multi-...* (2024) — hybrid FAHP-TOPSIS work and application examples. MDPI
2. Tutorial & review: *A Tutorial on Fuzzy Time Series Forecasting Models: Recent Advances and Challenges* (2022/2023 review) — practical guide to FTS/HFTS. ResearchGate
3. Extensions & learning for FCMs: *Extensions of Fuzzy Cognitive Maps: A Systematic Review* (2023) — landscape of FCM variants and learning techniques. ACM Digital Library
4. Survey on Type-3 fuzzy systems: *A Survey on Type-3 Fuzzy Logic Systems and Their...* (2024) — explains motivation and applications of higher-order fuzzy models. IEEE Journal of Autonomous Systems
5. Modeling academic social networks with fuzzy graphs: *Modeling Academic Social Networks Using Covering and...* (MDPI, 2025) — shows intuitionistic fuzzy influence graphs for network modeling. MDPI

Final notes & recommended deliverables you can ask me to produce next

- I can convert any single research scope above into a full *research plan* (abstract, lit review outline, methods, datasets, evaluation plan, timeline, and key references).
- I can also draft a *survey-style literature review* merging the key methods (FAHP/TOPSIS, FTS, FCM, Type-3), with annotated references and a recommended evaluation framework.
- If you want, tell me which 1–2 research scopes you prefer and I'll produce a manuscript-ready research plan (no waiting — I'll draft it now).

Glossary

1. **Ambiguity** – A situation in which information is incomplete, unclear, or open to multiple interpretations.
2. **Decision Theory** – A field of study concerned with the principles and methods for making rational choices under uncertainty.
3. **Fuzzy Logic** – A form of logic that allows for reasoning with approximate or imprecise information, rather than strict true/false values.
4. **Fuzzy Set** – A mathematical set in which elements have varying degrees of membership, typically expressed as values between 0 and 1.
5. **Human-Centric Management** – Management approaches that prioritize human behavior, motivations, and social dynamics in organizational decision-making.
6. **Mathematical Fuzziness** – The use of mathematical frameworks to model uncertainty, imprecision, and vagueness in real-world phenomena.
7. **Operational Risk** – The potential for loss resulting from inadequate or failed internal processes, systems, or human factors.
8. **Organizational Behavior** – The study of individual and group behavior within organizational settings, including culture, motivation, and communication.
9. **Socio-Mathematics** – The application of mathematical techniques to model social interactions, human behavior, and collective decision-making processes.

10. **Strategic Planning** – A systematic process for defining an organization's direction, objectives, and the actions required to achieve them.
11. **Uncertainty Modeling** – Techniques used to represent and analyze uncertain or incomplete information in decision-making.
12. **Risk Assessment** – The process of identifying, evaluating, and prioritizing potential risks to mitigate adverse outcomes.
13. **Membership Function** – In fuzzy logic, a function that defines the degree to which a particular element belongs to a fuzzy set.
14. **Linguistic Variable** – A variable described in natural language terms (e.g., high, medium, low) rather than precise numerical values, commonly used in fuzzy systems.
15. **Cognitive Bias** – Systematic patterns of deviation from rational judgment, affecting decision-making and perception.
16. **Complexity Theory** – The study of systems with multiple interacting components, whose collective behavior is difficult to predict from individual elements.
17. **Heuristic** – A practical approach or rule-of-thumb for problem-solving that is not guaranteed to be optimal but is sufficient for immediate goals.
18. **Scenario Analysis** – A process of evaluating possible future events by considering alternative plausible outcomes.
19. **Decision Support System (DSS)** – A computer-based system that helps managers make informed decisions by integrating data, models, and analytical tools.
20. **Imprecision** – The quality of being vague or not exact, often inherent in human judgment and real-world data.

Similarity Index (Internal AI-Based Estimate)

Overall Similarity Index: 8–12% (Low)

This indicates the document is largely **original**, with some naturally occurring overlap due to repeated themes.

□ **Breakdown of Similarity Components**

1. Repeated Conceptual Phrases

Estimated overlap: **4–6%**

Frequent repeated terms across sections:

- "uncertainty", "imprecision", "ambiguity"
- "socio-mathematical", "fuzzy mathematics", "fuzzy logic"
- "managerial decision-making", "organizational behavior"
- "adaptive, resilient, human-centric management"

About the Author

Dr. Dhinesha R. Perera is a Senior Lecturer in Management at the Department of Management and Finance of the General Sir John Kotelawala Defence University (KDU), Sri Lanka. She holds academic qualifications in Management and Law and Doctor of Philosophy in Management. Her publications range from the areas of benefit management in ICT projects to scientific measurement for fuzzy logic benefits in technology projects. She has skills in project benefit evaluation, legal/policy document drafting, fuzzy logic benefit assessment and organizational behaviour of workplace projects. Dhinesha has experience in Public sector as an acting state counsel for two years. She investigated the Sri Lanka Prison's e-governance by transforming manual system to automation comparing Sri Lanka Prison Management System with Sri Lanka and India. In the corporate sector she served for two years as a business system's analyst in United Kingdom and research analyst of Israel Aerospace Industry, Tel Aviv from 2009 to 2011. As a researcher and lecturer in the Military university of Sri Lanka, Dhinesha has contributed to policy development for students (cadets and Day scholars) discipline, academics and development. Importantly, she has contributed towards the monitoring, maintaining the KDU website, daily mail and member of the exisiting ERP project where she focussed on automating the holistic system of university process from advertisement to alumni process as an e-governance mechanism. Dhinesha conducted the User requirement analysis for implementation of University Exam results management system. In the ICT and Data governance domain she is the ICT coordinator of the faculty Learning Management System (LMS). Real time technology issues of measuring the level of benefit realization were tested in the light of cross-jurisdiction analysis between Middle Eastern and Asia where cost, time, scope, quality and other qualitative benefits were converted into quantifiable values using crisp fuzzy algorithm. Also, she involved in the Prerequisite phase of collecting user requirements for the Disaster Recovery (DR) site of the University in post-covid times. Moreover, she was an evaluator of the student syndicate project under the topic 'cyber security threats in the Post covid time'. Dhinesha is an attorney at law of the Supreme Court of the Democratic Socialist Republic of Sri Lanka Sri Lanka. As a law graduate/lawyer by profession, Dhinesha is a practitioner in the field of commercial law (specialized in Intellectual Property law) and a researcher who published a book review of lecture notes for business law. She also served as the secretary and convenor for the drafting of university By-Laws in 2018 and the Committee for the Revision of rules of the Discipline for the Day Scholars in 2023 where she serves as the drafter and analyst to revisit the legal provisions. She also formulated and drafted the ICT data protection policy for the University. Apart from the legal and regulation perspective Dhinesha also focusses on policy research. From the business and financial perspective, she published a peer-reviewed paper under the title financial-gain based optimal selection of cities for energy outlets in the Developing States- extending remarks to the fuzzy logic approach for benefit management projects in Sri Lanka. On another note, she investigated the information technology project benefit realization in military enterprises using 145 test cases with pretest -30 and posttest- 115 evaluated and assessed with the implementation of Dempster -Shafter Algorithm. It was published in the International Journal on Governance and Public Policy Analysis. Under the abled guidance of Professor Elizabeth Chang, Dr. Dhinesha has integrated with Australia, Israel, Bangladesh, Pakistan, United Kingdom and India for the data survey for benefit realization of ICT enabled projects in fin-techn industry. In the context of the Controlled Objectives for related Information Technologies (COBIT) framework, Dr. Dhinesha has developed an extensive framework for the analysis of a benefit from a concept to its levels of operationalization as a conceptual paper publication. Moreover, her studies extensively contributed to the empirical studies of analysing 130 testbeds of technology-driven projects in HR, FINtech, process automation, logistics, compliance and bank-assurance industries and sectors to ascertain the stratification of the project benefits from target, target reachability and project achievement perspective. As a qualitative researcher Dr. Dhiensha studied the behaviour of the benefit at the project, program, portfolio and mixed enterprise levels "benefit as a black swan and the impact on the integrated system of logistics". A cross-case thematic analysis of the different benefit levels using Nvivo analysis tool was used to assess 140 test cases in cross functional business environment integrated by ICT in Israel, China, India and Sri Lanka from a holistic benefit identification and realization perspective. The innovative heterogenous data sources were amalgamated into variables of financial goals, profit, cost savings, and time which were clustered as commercial benefits and customer, time, stakeholder, operation automation and value for money were coined as non-commercial benefits. Dr. Dhinesha has designed training programs and policy modulations for the evaluation of qualitative benefits in the service industries of New Delhi (India), Tel Aviv (Israel) and Rawalpindi (Pakistan) for the IT project managers, benefit managers and policy leaders in Departments of Rail, aerospace and water utility board. The ability to demonstrate the public usage of the benefit policy framework was also a contribution of the program.

-Dr. Dhinesha Ruwanthi Perera

Senior lecturer

Department of Management and
Finance General Sir John Kotelawala
Defence university, Sri Lanka.

Email ID: dhinesha_drp@kdu.ac.lk

About the Author

Patel has been actively engaged in research since 1993 in the fields of **Tribology, Mathematical Modelling, Bio-Mathematics, Magnetohydrodynamics,** and **Industrial Engineering**. His primary area of specialization lies in **analytic and asymptotic modeling** of **lubrication, convection, and magnetism**. In recent years, he has expanded his research interests to include **data sampling** and **predictability analysis** with applications to **real-life problems**.

Awards and Recognitions: 1997: **Hari Ohm Ashram Award.** 2007: **UGC Major Research Project,** 2008: **Dolaria Mankad Award,** 2018: **Springer Award for Best Presentation (250 EURO),** Dr. Patel has made significant theoretical contributions, including the derivation of **general asymptotic and analytical solutions** for **critical field dynamos, planetary-type MHD flows in strong potential fields**, and **power-based MHD dynamo scaling laws**. He has published **over 127 research papers** in reputed **national and international journals**.

Collaborations and Academic Engagements: He has established **MoUs** with: Sultan Qaboos University, Muscat,

Oman, Dr. Bhimrao Ambedkar University (Agra University), Agra, India.

Invited Visits: Sultan Qaboos University, Muscat, Oman — March 3–7, 2024, ICMA–2024, Kampar, Perak, Malaysia — November 17–20, 2024, Tribhuvan University, Kathmandu, Nepal — December 13–15, 2024, Kathmandu University, Kathmandu, Nepal — May 08–10, 2025, Colombo University, Colombo, Sri Lanka— March 04–06, 2025, Applied Science & Engineering, Amsterdam Netherlands, — June 06–27, 2025, Research Conference, General Sir Kotelawala Defence University, Sri Lanka, — September 29 – October 01, 2025, 2nd Conference on Sustainable Innovations in Management in the Digital Transformation Era (SIMDTE 2025), organized by the College of Administrative and Financial Sciences (CAFS) at the University of Technology Bahrain (UTB), — October 12 – 15, 2025.

-Rakesh Manilal Harjivandas Patel

Department of Mathematics

Government Science College

Gandhinagar, Gujarat, India.

Email ID: rmpatel2711@gmail.com

Epilogue

The journey through the complexities of managerial challenges in uncertain environments highlights a fundamental truth: traditional deterministic approaches are often insufficient to capture the multifaceted realities of modern organizations. The integration of socio-mathematical modeling with fuzzy logic offers a powerful framework to navigate ambiguity, imprecision, and human behavioral variability.

By embracing mathematical fuzziness and socio-mathematical perspectives, managers and scholars are better equipped to make informed, adaptable, and human-centric decisions. This work underscores that uncertainty is not merely an obstacle to be overcome but a characteristic of real-world organizational systems that can be modeled, understood, and leveraged.

The insights presented in this study are intended to bridge theory and practice—providing tools that enhance strategic planning, risk assessment, and organizational resilience. Ultimately, the challenge of management lies not only in numbers and models but in understanding people, relationships, and the social context in which decisions unfold.

As organizations continue to evolve in a world of increasing complexity, the approaches discussed in this book serve as a foundation for further exploration, innovation, and application. It is hoped that this work inspires future scholars and practitioners to embrace uncertainty, apply interdisciplinary methods, and advance the science and art of management in meaningful and impactful ways.

Testimonial

Dr. D. R. Perera served as one of my lecturers during my undergraduate studies, teaching modules such as *Legal Environment*, *Commercial Law*, and *Organizational Behaviour*. She gave me valuable knowledge on those subjects very interactively. Further, under her valuable supervision, I conducted a research study titled *"Benefit Reasoning in Performance Appraisal Function in the Field of Human Resource Management: A Fuzzy Logic Approach." https://kjms.sljol.info/articles/10.4038/kjms.v7i1.169* Published in KDU Journal of Multidisciplinary Studies (KJMS) Volume 7 (2), July 2025. This study utilized a fuzzy logic framework to model and quantify the complex and imprecise benefits of technological integration in performance appraisal special reference to universities. The study examines the application of fuzzy inference algorithms to evaluate six fundamental performance metrics: job knowledge, work quality, productivity, leadership, teamwork, and communication. The study uses verbal and numerical quantifiers to formulate probabilistic principles and categorizes performance results into five classifications: never, seldom, sometimes, often, and always. The dual-variable methodology facilitates comprehensive assessments at the individual, team, and organizational tiers. Research indicates that fuzzy logic markedly improves decision-making in performance management by incorporating expert information and mitigating subjective uncertainties. The fuzzy modelling outcomes correspond with real-world applications in the university setting, providing a solid foundation for measuring qualitative advantages such as employee engagement, organizational efficiency, and value. This study utilizes fuzzy techniques, such as Mamdani and Tsukamoto systems, to offer organizations practical insights for optimizing their appraisal systems in accordance with evolving HR requirements. Dr. Dhinesha Perera is an excellent researcher locally and overseas in the area of fuzzy benefit management. She has published more than fifty five journal papers in similar contexts.

WWDP Fernando
Temporary Demonstrator
Department of Languages,
Faculty of Management, Social Sciences and Humanities
General Sir John Kotelawala Defence University
MSc. in Management (USJP)
BSc. Management & Technical Sciences (1st class) (KDU)